# THE DARKNESS
## PERMISSION TO ROCK!
### the unofficial book

## JASON ARNOPP

# CONTENTS

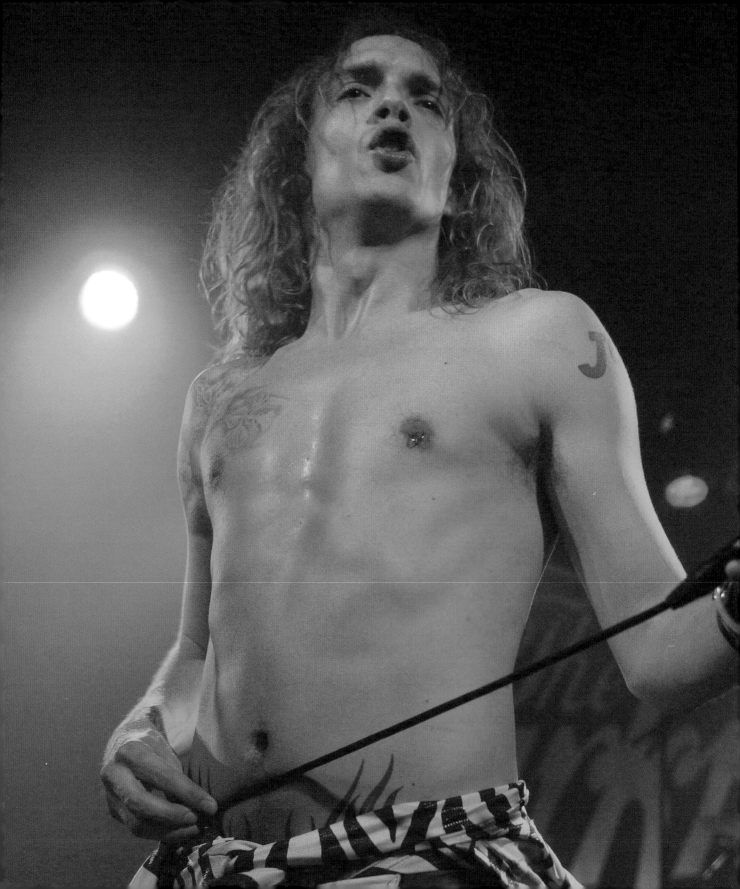

# HELL'S BELLS

When Justin Hawkins awoke on the morning of 25 December 2003, Santa had truly delivered. His band, The Darkness, were sitting pretty at Number 2 in the UK charts with a festive rock single 'Christmas Time (Don't Let the Bells End)'. Justin couldn't decide what was more rewarding: that he and his bandmates had scored with a rampant Yuletide tune, or the fact that they had cunningly smuggled the phrase 'bell end' into the hit parade.

As he had predicted, the single's chart performance was 'the cherry on the cake of our year'. A lot of work had been required to set it up, but 2003 had been the most thrillingly hectic twelve months of the band members' lives. They had headlined three UK tours – including their pre-Christmas run of Elf Hazard dates – and visited America for live shows, which suggested bigger things were in store for them. They appeared on the bill of almost every major UK festival. They released three singles, which had progressively scaled the charts, boosted by increasingly outrageous videos. They unleashed their debut album *Permission To Land* through the major label East West, knocking pop diva Beyoncé Knowles off the Number 1 spot and outstripping the likes of those cherished Brit ambassadors Coldplay in terms of sales growth.

The record had sold well over 700,000 copies, making it double-platinum in the UK. Perhaps their biggest achievement of all had been to make rock 'n' roll fun again. They had successfully launched a fearless rock band who had no interest in depressing you with tales of troubled childhoods or urban deprivation. Instead, they were a band who enticed audiences to stick their thumbs in the air; a band who made you grin like a fool while rocking you like a hurricane; a band who actually affirmed life, as opposed to slinging nihilistic mud pies at it.

The Darkness were now the biggest band in Britain. Justin, his guitarist brother Dan, bassist Frankie Poullain and drummer Ed Graham would get mobbed wherever they went, by fans who had been nicknamed Darklings. Even the band's security guard hadn't seen anything like this, during his twenty years in the business. Men in white vans would yell abuse at them while passing, which was always the mark of becoming a household name in this country.

Some aspects of the year had been testing: Justin's throat was worn ragged by twelve months of shrieking like an agonised wildebeest, and he didn't leave his north London home much any more. An internal bust-up, at one point along the road to success, had left an imperceptible fracture mark in the quartet's unity. Yet no one could say that the present end didn't justify the means: besides the joy of carving their initials into rock's history books and receiving recognition for their years of stubborn, lonely toil, The Darkness would likely become millionaires by the end of 2004.

These four men mostly hailed from Lowestoft. It was a small easterly Suffolk outpost, famous to sneering outsiders for its liability to pop up in conversation, whenever a handy example of a dead town was required. At the start of 2003, the man on the street didn't know these people from Adam & the Ants. Yet here were Lowestoft's favourite sons, strutting like peacocks across every TV screen in the UK, in the flash video for their Christmas hit.

Across the country, nonbelievers' jaws struck floors. You couldn't have made this up. Unless, of course, you were Justin Hawkins.

'I taught myself how to play guitar
I was on a mission'

'He's not scared to
try anything — nothing

# Chapter 1
# UNLEASHED IN THE EAST

*'Woooaaaaaaaaaa!'* The year was 1990 and Justin Hawkins was screaming his lungs out for a select audience of one – an audience sitting in a separate room. Standing in the bath enjoying a shower, Justin howled his way through a not-so-subtle combination of personally invented songs and rock standards. His friend and bandmate James Leah sat in an adjacent room, marvelling at the vertiginous nature of the notes being struck. Any minute now, thought Leah, a posse of stray dogs might come bounding into the house, answering the Hawkins call.

'It was hideous,' recalls Leah today. 'I'd never heard anything like it before, and haven't again since. I don't think Justin could go that high now – if he did, he'd be in the record books and kids everywhere would hurt themselves trying to copy him.'

The two teenagers had met only recently, after joining a new local rock band named Biff. Leah was waiting at the Hawkinse's family home to pick his friend up for band practice. Justin and his younger siblings Dan and Suzi had been born in Chertsey, Surrey. Their Londoner parents shifted them to Saxmundham and Darsham, before finally migrating here to a pleasant Lowestoft suburb, Carlton Colville.

With a population of roughly sixty thousand people, Lowestoft is Britain's most easterly town, featuring an award-winning beach and a slowly ailing fish industry. To grow up here was to be surrounded by greenery, cliffs, buckets and spades. The North Sea was rarely more than fifteen minutes away for a Lowestoft kid. The town's crime rate has risen dramatically post-millennium, but these were once leafy paths and streets that you could explore without fear of being pummelled into submission.

Wearing rock T-shirts, tight jeans and growing his hair long was never going to see Justin filed under 'cool' at the start of the nineties. 'I've always chosen to listen to stuff that everything else thought wasn't cool,' he later said. 'It feels a bit more personal to me'. Mainstream pop folk, with their Saturday night shirts and single earrings, were never going to connect with Justin, and even the rock world was about to undergo redecoration. Nirvana unleashed 'Smells Like Teen Spirit' and popularised grunge music – a genre that was at once a culling of rock's more ludicrous excesses and its life-affirming thrills.

Whether you liked it or not, grunge made joining a band seem within the grasp of mortals. Most of the genre's icons looked like people you might bump into at the supermarket. The ability to play flash, endless guitar solos was no longer a requisite – grunge bands proudly flaunted an anti-rock-star vibe.

Establishing the habit of a lifetime, Justin had gone directly against the grain by absorbing a year's worth of guitar tuition, practising for up to eight times the number of hours set for him as homework. He later claimed that, by the end of that twelve months, he ended up surpassing his teacher.

Justin would reflect that his guitar playing benefited from the fact that he wasn't part of the in-crowd. Not for him, sitting under the local Claremont Pier and indulging in shady practices with cool kids. 'Instead, I was in my bedroom playing guitar like a motherf****r. It's worked out for me now, so I'm not bitter in any way. But I think it goes some way to explaining who I am.'

He was the last person to join Biff, answering a local newspaper advert placed by the band's guitarist Steve Hobbs, requesting a guitarist who could perform backing vocals. Already in place were the aforementioned James Leah, Steve's drumming brother Dan and singer Craige Wilson. By the time the scrawny fifteen-year-old Justin arrived at the Hobbs house with his impressive Charvel guitar, the band had already played a few rehearsals. It was a potentially intimidating scenario for a rock 'n' roll novice, but Justin showed no signs of cracking. Instead, he switched into motormouth mode.

'Justin was doing all the talking,' says Leah, recalling his first impressions. 'He was telling cheesy jokes – I don't think Steve and the others were really into it. They weren't sure whether to keep him on. Because I liked Justin, I wanted to tell him not to try so hard, but I never did. In the end, they kept him on anyway.'

Besides being impressed by Justin's extrovert personality, and his Charvel, Leah noted that the boy played a 'mean solo, with big distortion'. Biff largely played other people's songs: sped-up versions of the Beatles' 'Lucy in the Sky with Diamonds', Deee-Lite's 'Groove Is in the Heart' and the Cult's 'Lil Devil', to name but a few. Nineteen ninety-one saw the band record two demo tapes at Lowestoft's Beech Tree Farm Studio, featuring tunes such as 'Don't Go Down in the Cellar' and 'Trouble Being Myself'. On the second demo, the strongest aspect of the three songs is arguably Justin's accomplished guitar solo on 'Shooting a Star'. Yet strangely, despite the teen's shower-shaking vocal talents, he didn't sing in the band.

James Leah came to realise that there was far more to Justin than the nerd persona that the media would later attribute to him. 'He's not really a geek,' says Leah. 'He plays the geek in an ironic way, but he's a really outgoing character. Pretty fearless, too. He's not scared to try anything – nothing intimidates him. He'll use his silliness to get around people.'

Justin didn't experience the crippling fear of girls that afflicts most paid-up geeks. Far from it. 'I used to watch him chat up girls,' says one friend. 'He'd go up to them and they'd ignore him but end up going out with him anyway. He even had a book of a hundred and one chat-up lines, which used to work quite well. I thought, This guy's got style!'

# 'Justin
### *was always a star*'

While Frankie Poullain – the son of a classical musician, who later became a pilot – was practising his bass guitar in a tiny Scottish village named Milnathort, his future bandmates all attended Lowestoft's Kirkley High School. Studying and socialising alongside the Hawkins brothers was Ed Graham, born ten miles away in Great Yarmouth. A relatively mellow soul, keen on fishing, bird watching and wildlife in general, Graham was nicknamed Badger by schoolmates, due to white patches on his eyebrows. No wonder he was so fond of hitting things with big sticks. Justin, meanwhile, was nicknamed Y-Fronts Man, due to his occasional fondness for wearing his underwear outside his trousers.

While the vast majority of pupils made noncommittal noises in the presence of career advisers, the exceptionally driven Dan Hawkins had already made important life decisions. 'I knew from an early age exactly what I wanted to do,' he has said. 'I wanted to be a musician and that was it. It made life a lot easier, knowing what I was aiming for. I taught myself how to play guitar. I was on a mission.'

Justin continued to be one of the school's token rock outcasts. Having been inspired chiefly by Aerosmith's frontman Steven Tyler since the band's *Pump* album emerged in 1989, Justin would wear silk scarves akin to those of his hero. 'I don't necessarily remember people taking the mickey out of him,' says Kirkley High's deputy headmistress, Hazel Johnson, 'because whatever was said to him, he'd have a quick retort. I got the impression that he had a very clear sense of direction. There appeared to be something slightly different about him – and I'm not surprised that he writes music and is highly creative.'

Studying a couple of years below this man of rock, Ed and Dan were more into the likes of the Cure, the Pixies and My Bloody Valentine – bands seen as far cooler than, say, Justin's beloved Van Halen. Ed's house became a centre of operations for any number of fledgling groups, which would generally crumble almost as soon as they had finished writing their first song.

The first band Ed formed at Kirkley High featured around eight people and remained nameless. The posse specialised in covers by Ned's Atomic Dustbin and the Sisters of Mercy. Their social life, like most alternative-minded kids, revolved around the Fighting Cocks pub or Forbes Brewery – a fine bar, which began life as a glorified barn with bales of hay masquerading as seats. If you appeared too young to get served at these drinkeries, you'd have to socialise at Colville House Youth Club, sip your Coke and watch the local skaters.

When his eight-man band inevitably dissolved, Ed noted that Dan Hawkins had left a band called Vital Signs and sought his musical collaboration. The result was Superfuzz Bigmuff, blatantly named after grunge mob Mudhoney's recently released debut EP. They mostly played My Bloody Valentine covers and were, according to band member Greg Moore, 'a complete wall of noise' when they played their one and only gig, at Colville House. Audience member John King remembers them as being, 'pretty good, actually. When we were at school, almost everyone seemed to be into My Bloody Valentine. That's why I was so surprised when The Darkness ended up being such a rock band!'

King notes that Superfuzz Bigmuff was 'the only whole band I remember Ed forming. He was constantly working with other musicians, but nothing really took off.' Ed and Dan subsequently wrote some reportedly 'cracking' songs together, but these were heard by few people outside of Ed's bedroom.

There had yet to be any musical interaction between the Hawkins brothers, save a little nascent jamming when their very cool dad bought them equipment as kids. 'Dan and Justin argued a lot,' says Greg Moore. 'Justin was into rock stuff, whereas Dan was more indie. Me and Dan would go to Forbes or the Fighting Cocks, but we'd never really hang out with Justin.'

Justin later told *Kerrang!* magazine, 'Before The Darkness, Dan and I couldn't see eye to eye with each other about anything. We certainly couldn't have played together in a band. I was a bit of a geeky rocker. Dan's always had a bit more of a 'cool'-ness about him. He probably had no desire to be in a band with me because I was such a twat. I think those are the same reasons it's working so well now.'

'Justin was always a star,' said Dan, 'at school or family gatherings. And a total pain in the arse as a kid.' Justin would come to consider his OTT performance with The Darkness a valve for his hyperactive behaviour. 'Having been a bit of a clown at school,' he mused, 'it's nice to have that out of my system. Rather than sitting in a classroom full of people trying to learn who're saying, "Stop being such a c**t", I'm up there.'

Justin, Dan and especially Ed would infuriate teachers and pupils alike by rhythmically tapping on their desks. Ed's maths teacher would refer to him as 'Ringo'. Even his lovably perky English teacher David Butcher was driven to distraction by the trio's perniciously percussive behaviour. Says Hazel Johnson, 'Staff now fondly remember them for that tapping. Ed in particular would really enjoy a good drum during lessons. I think his own mother, who was a teacher, quite honestly despaired that he would ever get anywhere!'

Nevertheless, the trio did well in their GCSEs, marking them out as the

most infuriating of pupils: those who mess about, but still rake in the grades. Says Hazel Johnson, 'They were not without some considerable ability. I'm not saying they ever fully realised their potential in school, because I don't think they did, and school was probably not the greatest thing for someone like Justin. But, judging by things I've heard, he remembers it quite fondly.'

Interestingly, none of our three megastars-in-waiting took up music as a subject option during their time at Kirkley. 'One can only say', notes Hazel Johnson, 'that Justin learned his writing skills through his own efforts. He had a very clear desire to be different. You can see that today, from the costume and all the rest of it now. He's very much an individualist.'

'He was really quite clever,' says history teacher Phil Spencer. 'I always felt he could achieve whatever he wanted to achieve. Justin Hawkins becoming a rock star doesn't surprise me at all.' Justin would tell Radio 1's *Lamacq Live*, 'The teachers used to call me an immature attention seeker. I can't imagine why! I just wanted to be entertaining. I just wanted to *flyyyy*!'

One of James Leah's abiding memories of his time in Biff is when he and Justin poked their heads up through the skylight of a mobile Fiat Punto owned by their drummer's mother. The pair were entertaining themselves by threatening to hurl Pot Noodles at utterly bamboozled pedestrians. 'They'd been heated and cooled down,' notes Leah, 'so they weren't dangerous.'

Then there was the time that the Biff guitarist Steve Hobbs accidentally drove his Sherpa van into a ditch in the middle of the Suffolk countryside, with the demonic duo sitting in the back. Leah remembers, 'Half the van went straight in. Steve had been going around a corner, so he must have dropped to about twenty miles per hour, but that's still quite fast. Justin just made jokes out of it – he wasn't very helpful at all!'

Hawkins and Leah seemed to have formed their own insular bond, finding constant delight in abstract, distinctly British humour. Justin's preferred comedy was, after all, Benny Hill, the *Carry On* films and seemingly anything involving half-naked women being chased by bald men at high speed. 'Most of the time in Biff,' says Leah, 'me and Justin just messed about, ignoring everybody. We were just bell ends and enjoyed being like that. No one else really wanted to join in.'

Biff's finest moment as a band arguably saw them play for two hundred people in a nightclub called the Zone, a stone's throw from the sea. 'That night,' says Leah, 'someone popped up with a contract. He wanted to buy the band, or something! I passed him on to Steve and never heard anything more about it.'

He and Justin may not have taken Biff particularly seriously, but they pined for the band when it finally dissolved, following an internal bust-up. 'Because we were playing cover versions, we weren't really that credible,' admits Leah, 'but it was a really fun time, just because of the company, and the antics we got up to. We were at a loose end after Biff.'

Needless to say, when Justin Hawkins found himself at a loose end, it didn't last for long.

'There's a *balance*
between them musically
that just works'

# Chapter 2

# TEENAGE KICKS

Jon Allen was a shade confused. Two local teenagers, ten years his junior, had turned up at his newly opened Soundhouse Studios in Lowestoft, asking if he fancied contributing drums to a creative musical session. So here the owner was, perched behind the kit and attempting to percussively drive one of the more ludicrous songs ever written. Justin Hawkins played guitar and sang, while James Leah played bass. Lyrically, the ditty concerned a man who went to market and somehow contrived to break both of his knees. Musically, it was a twisty, turny eel.

'The one thing obvious about Justin was that he was always going to be experimental in what he did,' recalls Allen. '*God*, was he experimental! You'd be sitting there playing the music and it would go off on a tangent. You'd think, Hold on a second! It was very, very strange.'

'There was some kind of lyrical hook based around the word "Hello",' says Leah, 'and a dramatic bit with a huge solo. Jon looked a bit bemused and uncomfortable, like he wasn't being let in on a joke. After a while, I don't think he wanted to play any more.'

This session exemplified the joys of teenage rocking. There was no particular mission statement, just sheer boundless creativity – albeit creativity to which few people on the globe would voluntarily listen.

'I don't really know why we did it,' admits Leah, 'because we didn't have any objectives, like being famous. We were just pissing about. Nothing came of that session at all, other than Jon thinking we were twats.'

At this point, Father Mahunga was Justin and James's chosen band name. Again, the fact that the latter has no idea how the name was spelled speaks volumes about the duo's carefree nature back then. The Mahunga experience had begun post-Biff and originally featured Ed Graham's cousin Paul, who preferred the moniker Treefrog for reasons that no one can recall. Again, the Hawkins/Leah combination proved testing for some. 'Treefrog got pissed off that me and Justin just wanted to do "Smells Like Teen Spirit" covers,' says Leah. 'I don't think Justin was into grunge as such – he just liked that song.'

Father Mahunga saw a procession of local musos come and go, eventually boiling down to the two men who pestered Jon Allen at the Soundhouse in 1993. The owner would also, on occasion, see Dan Hawkins. 'Dan was only starting out,' he says. 'He would come in and ask us to plug his gear in for him. Justin was a bit more accomplished, but they were both young, impressionable Lowestoft lads. I would say Justin was the stronger of the two and knew what he was doing and Dan was, to a degree, running along behind. He was serious, but he didn't know why.'

After The Darkness took off, Justin would tell *Guitar* magazine that Dan was 'a big, strong man with a solid heart full of gold. He's the driving force behind us. And I'm the peripheral show-off that makes it all a bit more glamorous.'

Justin eventually unveiled a live project of his own devising, which was tailor-made for showing off: Bionic Reg. This involved his appearing on stage in a purple superhero suit. On his head sat a plastic helmet with the letter 'R' on the front and what appeared to be a Sellotaped-on cardboard shark's fin poking up towards the ceiling. Justin – or Reg, if you will – would then play guitar, sing and/or roll around the stage, depending on his mood. One friend has memorably described Bionic Reg as 'the Les Dawson of rock 'n' roll', mainly because he would often deliberately play wrong notes.

Witnesses to the legend that was Bionic Reg speak of it with no little reverence. James Leah saw an early show at a packed Fighting Cocks pub, during which Justin welcomed six other musicians on stage for an impromptu brainstorm. 'Justin spread ketchup on himself to look like blood,' says Leah, 'and he had a huge cardboard cock tied to his guitar. After that, he thought it would be funnier if it was just him playing. Musically, Justin made it all up himself and included lots of guitar solos. It was cheese rock.' John King further recalls a Fighting Cocks show that saw Justin 'dressed as some kind of tree spirit' – a perfectly believable claim.

Jon Allen caught one of Justin's subsequent solo performances at the Lowestoft nightclub then known as Tuttles. Having opened his Soundhouse studio, he was investigating local talent and got more than he bargained for. 'It was unbelievable,' he says. 'Here was a guy who was prepared to do whatever it took to get where he was going to go. He's such an extrovert and his guitar playing was quite accomplished, but obviously not as good as he's doing now. The music was best described as avant-garde.'

Despite the deeply idiosyncratic nature of Bionic Reg, Allen claims he could discern Justin's star potential. 'I'm not surprised he's doing The Darkness now. You could easily have dismissed Justin – and I suppose you still could – as nothing but a showman, but you could tell he was serious about what he was doing.'

The Bionic Reg era was, presumably, the only one that saw Justin persuading a friend to fire ping-pong balls at him, pre-show, in order to warm him up. He also had some Bionic fun with his grandmother Dot one afternoon. After telling her that it was the law to wear a Bionic Reg helmet in a van, the pair drove around Lowestoft town centre modelling them. 'When she got out,' one observer remembers, 'she forgot she had it on and almost walked around Lowestoft town centre.'

Bionic Reg also made an appearance in one of Leah's college videos. Viewing this today, you'd find it very hard to reconcile the on-screen Justin Hawkins with the one we see pouting out of magazine spreads. Sporting his Reg outfit, complete with a few accessories dangling from the helmet, Justin hops wackily along a road clutching a rope, seemingly being pulled by a mysterious force. He meets a man in a karate costume and utters his one and only line, 'Could I have some directions, please?' Titled *Egg's 11* for no good reason, the two-minute video is very silly indeed, but undeniably carries a youthful spark and more than a nod to the abstract comedy of *Monty Python's Flying Circus*. Barely audible in the background is music co-written by James and Justin – the latter playing guitar and singing meaningless lyrics about spiders, elephants and the eighties comedian-pianist Richard Stilgoe.

Justin left Kirkley High School in 1993, while midway through his A levels. This was allegedly because he discovered he would have to stand up and talk to the rest of the class, as part of his history course. Strange reasoning indeed, from a man who would in later life address thousands of people at a time.

Justin hopped aboard a two-year media course at Lowestoft College. Meanwhile, at the age of seventeen, Dan Hawkins decided to abandon Lowestoft. 'I thought, f**k this, my grades are all really good, but I don't want to do this any more. Luckily, our parents were understanding enough to let us try for what we wanted.' Shifting operations to London, he set about

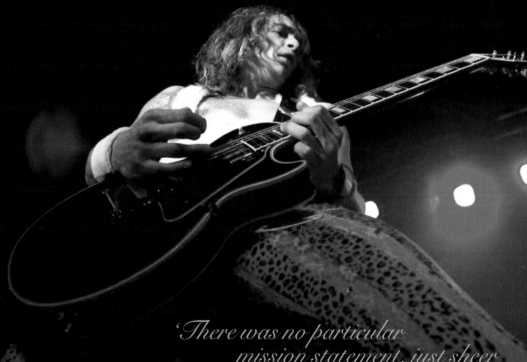

'There was no particular
mission statement, just sheer
*boundless creativity*'

'I am the peripheral show-off that makes it a bit more *glamorous*'

JUSTIN

placing adverts in newspapers, searching for like-minded souls. 'We were very impressed when he did that,' admits his friend Greg Moore. 'He would come back some weekends and tell us what he was up to.'

Dan and Justin's mother told Radio 1, 'Dan finally joined this band [in London], then proceeded to sack everyone! ... Daniel has always been the serious hardworking one ... Justin has just floated around and couldn't care less about anything much, including school.'

Attempting to present any definitive account of Justin's subsequent musical movements is a difficult task even for close friends, due in equal measure to his restlessly prolific nature and to the haphazard chaos of Lowestoft's music scene in the early nineties. That period is best summed up as fuelled by musical experimentation, incestuous band hopping and an indecent volume of Scrumpy Jack cider. Justin placed a big fat tick in all of the above boxes.

One of Justin's bands, which has people scratching their heads and offering vague recollections, is Lung Nugget, an apparently short-lived combo. James Leah recalls that his own band Mother Spin supported Lung Nugget at the Metro Club – a tiny place on the slightly dodgy Commercial Road, which leads down towards docks. 'Dan [Hawkins] was on drums,' he says. 'They were wearing silly costumes – they were definitely intending to be a comedy band, as the name suggested.'

Justin also spent time in a weird-rock posse named Fish Logic. Arguably his most serious proposition arrived when he lent some guitar-abuse to From Their Heads Came, a local industrial-rock band with a notably hard-edged, aggressive sound. The outfit, which featured Treefrog from Father Mahunga, was Justin's passport to performing his first shows beyond Lowestoft. They played gigs in Great Yarmouth and Norwich, even venturing as far afield as Cambridge and London. During this time, Justin is remembered primarily for having a 'huge' level of distortion on his guitar and showing the audience his behind during a Yarmouth show. Leah recalls, 'There was a photograph of that with light shining on him, so it looked like light was quite literally shining out of his arse.'

From Their Heads Came got progressively noisier. At one show in London's Euston, they were reportedly too loud for hecklers to make themselves heard. As a result, the band were handed pieces of paper bearing unflattering, handwritten messages. The head-banging fraternity, on the other hand, were loving it.

Even at this point, James Leah doesn't believe his friend wanted to be a rock star. 'We never talked about plans at all. We were too busy joking around. I didn't sense the whole attitude of wanting to make it, no matter what – he just really liked music and wanted to have a laugh. He was a creative person, and those people don't think about fame and money – that stuff comes out as a side effect of what they do.'

'If you look at The Darkness now,' offers the Soundhouse's Jon Allen, 'Justin hasn't actually changed. His singing style and everything are the same – he's just got older. And he's where he should be.'

*'Once you meet him, you never forget him'*

# Chapter 3
# I WANT TO BREAK FREE

There's a song on The Darkness's 2003 debut album *Permission To Land* called 'Stuck in a Rut'. Featuring lines such as 'No more to rot in this sty, turn my back on this shithole in the blink of an eye', it was reportedly inspired by the situation in which Justin Hawkins found himself after dropping out of Lowestoft College, midway through his media course. Having moved from Carlton Colville to live with his girlfriend in a house owned by his dad, this creative dynamo suddenly found himself tucked away on Lowestoft's West Bevan Street. This was a slightly desolate part of town where small businesses continually seemed to spring up, only to wilt through lack of attention. There was always the worry that it might have the same effect on stimulus-hungry people like Justin. Now on the dole, he had finally become disillusioned about playing in bands. 'Grunge was depressing,' he later said. 'I liked Nirvana, but everything that happened after it was rubbish. So I decided I wanted to learn about music technology and computers and acoustics.'

The Lowestoft College course had introduced Justin to the possibilities of musical technology, specifically concerning keyboards and midi sequencers. His ever-helpful father bought him some equipment, including an Atari ST computer and Q-Bass software. Justin set everything up in the flat's spare room and waited for inspiration. After all, there was plenty of time to kill.

'Sometimes, Justin would call me up,' says James Leah, 'and ask me to come over and hear these new songs he'd written on his keyboard. One day, he had this really cool piece of music on which he sang. It sounded like a cross between Michael Jackson and Ministry. He played it at [the Lowestoft nightclub] City Lights in the disco and people started dancing around on the stage, like it was an official piece of music. I really loved that song and I still think about it … I don't think it even had a name.'

Occasionally, Justin would apply for a job. He took a stab at becoming one of Great Yarmouth's many bingo callers. Then he approached Pontin's holiday camp in Lowestoft, answering an advert for an Elvis Presley impersonator. He would undoubtedly have pulled it off – despite not particularly liking Elvis – but his dreadlocks possibly guaranteed his rejection.

Friends started to feel a little sorry for Justin, as he sat there watching daytime TV, often working out how to play the various cheesy theme tunes and jingles that blared out of the box. He developed a liking for anthems. Operating under the superb project name Organzola, he and James Leah

created 'The West Bevan Street Albion Theme'. This was named after a football team in which Justin played alongside various pals at Lowestoft Sports Centre every Sunday.

While it may have seemed that Justin was frittering away his existence, jingles – and to a lesser extent football – would play key roles in his life over the next few years.

Rick Cocker is the man who interviewed The Darkness's future frontman for a place at Huddersfield Technical College in 1995. Justin applied for a two-year B-Tech course, hopefully culminating in a National Diploma in Music Technology. 'He spoke very well and was very polite,' says Cocker. 'That was one of the first things that impressed me about him. He was obviously still interested in composition, but his main interest was recording and what computers could do.'

Justin got the slot and prepared to move to Huddersfield for the course's September start. Unlike universities, the college didn't offer live-in accommodation, or even a student bar. Justin would have to find his own social life and, more fundamentally, his own flat. Luckily, he had a Lowestoft friend in mind, with whom to make the move.

Justin's Kirkley High schoolmate Greg Moore returned from working in America in the summer of 1995. 'I gave Justin a call and he told me about the course,' says Moore. 'He suggested that I join the course and form a band with him. And I did.'

Come September, the pair found themselves sharing a £17.50-per-week bedroom in a flat that Moore considered 'an absolute shithole'. Among the varied fruits of their labours on the course was a twenty-minute camcorder film named *The Methane Switchboard*. 'We spent six months on it,' laughs Moore. 'It was about tenants living in a post-apocalyptic bedsit complex. Justin played a martial arts expert called Soft Lad. The house was powered by methane, via a "methane terminal", which was the bathroom. Typical student humour.'

There was also much typical student behaviour. The flat would often play host to boozy parties, including a pancake-dominated bash. 'There were about a hundred pancakes,' chuckles Greg Moore, 'and it turned into a huge food fight. Then people start puking up everywhere.' Come the weekend, Hawkins and Moore would put on their jazzy nylon shirts and hit a crazy joint such as Bradford's Cheesus Christ, which was situated above a workingmen's club. 'We'd get down to a bit of Northern Soul,' says Moore. 'It was good fun: we'd get shit-faced on cheap beer.'

Justin often earned straight distinctions on his college course, which was nurturing his innate ability to write accomplished tunes. 'He would spend most of his time composing jingles,' says Moore. 'He was really good at it, and he had a laugh doing it. He got a lot of praise for what he was writing.'

'The music he was working on was very retrograde,' judges Rick Cocker. 'I wouldn't say his stuff became a joke, because he was too good to be a joke. His jingles were brilliant – they were extremely well composed, incredibly catchy and you'd hear them all bloody day long. Six months later, you were still able to hum this stuff.'

Justin's easy-listening fetish grew apace, as he emulated various sixties sounds and Hammond organ *fromage* aplenty. 'He sent me a tape of some good stuff he'd done,' says James Leah. 'It was a little like the Cardiacs.' On this tape was Justin's interpretation of the theme tune from Matthew Kelly's TV game show *Going For Gold*, plus original songs such as 'The Glory of Parisian Architecture', 'The Flag & Hat Marquee' and, perhaps his all-time finest song title, 'How Much Fun Can You Have For a Pound (Nowadays)'. Listening to this tape today, you'd think it incredible that its creator would go on to front a band like The Darkness. If you're thinking that Justin Hawkins is somehow less credible as a result, however, then consider this: easy-listening music, in its own way, is just as extreme and unfashionable as classic rock.

The band that Justin and Greg Moore formed at Huddersfield was named Captain Centipede. Justin wrote all the songs and performed guitar and vocals, with Moore on drums and a bass player called James. Among the interestingly named tunes on offer were 'Martyr of the Meat Crisis', 'Old Man's Jukebox' and 'Brian May'. 'One of the college lecturers owned a publishing company and said he'd consider offering us a deal.'

A nice idea, but it was not to be. That summer, Hawkins and Moore returned to Lowestoft and started playing music with Ed Graham. Then Greg received a call from America: he was urgently needed back there for work. Realising that the Huddersfield course hadn't truly fulfilled him, Moore reluctantly took his halfway-house diploma and crossed the Atlantic. 'I was really sorry to leave,' he says, genuinely. 'Justin's a pretty special guy – once you meet him, you never forget him. I admire his morals – he loves his family to bits and he's a really loyal friend.'

Undeterred by Captain Centipede's demise beneath fate's hobnailed boot, Justin was determined to enjoy the summer. He went camping at the Reading Festival – this was something he did for several years, perhaps unaware that in the near future he'd be leaping about on that stage himself. On the campsite, Justin and Ed would frequently organise what they liked to label the Fun Centre. This comprised a circle of tents and a lengthy conga line. 'It was built around the foundation of very heavy drinking,' Justin later said. 'We had power-drinking competitions wearing a special cape – which was really a pink blanket – while standing in the most macho way you could.' One night, Justin made everyone in the tent circle deliver a speech. When one man sincerely told the group that the Fun Centre meant a lot to him, as he didn't have many friends, there was hardly a dry eye in the field.

Justin's second year at the college, during which he lived in Halifax, saw him making real progress. 'He was certainly achieving more,' judges Rick Cocker. 'The general feeling was that he would go far – but not necessarily in the way that he went. I thought he was very likely to do well as a commercial writer for the media.'

One of Justin's major projects, towards the end of the course, was a rock opera. 'It was more of a drums-and-guitar affair,' says Cocker. 'It had a story, with a plot. The music had themes running through it to dramatise the storyline. He sang, but we weren't particularly aware of his falsetto in those days.' Hawkins would earn one distinction for his opera, then more for 'composition and arrangement' and the more cryptically titled 'managing and developing self'. 'Basically,' summarises Cocker, 'he demonstrated to all lecturers that he had the ability to see a project through. Tying that in with his composition skills, that's why we thought Justin was most likely to succeed, of all our students.'

Emerging from his two-year stint with flying colours, Justin settled down for several celebratory pints with his colleagues and lecturers. 'One of the things I jokingly said to him', laughs Cocker, 'was not to forget us when he's rich and famous, and we'll have the Justin Hawkins Studio. Sure enough, he phoned me up last week and said, "I suppose you want to know about the Justin Hawkins Studio." So he remembered. And I want to pursue that one!'

By all accounts, Huddersfield was a real milestone for Justin Hawkins. 'It was a turning point in his life,' believes James Leah. 'He learned how to play as a more technically knowledgeable musician. He gathered a good portfolio to present to people who wanted music for adverts.'

Rather than return to Lowestoft, Justin headed straight for London's smog, where he slept on people's sofas in the Shepherd's Bush area, before living in Angel with his brother Dan and Frankie Poullain. To support his endless quest for a stable, viable band, industrious Dan held a day job, which at least positioned him in the music business: he was a receptionist at Rondor, the now defunct record company. Owned by the brass deity Herb Alpert, it had once signed the Sex Pistols for approximately one week in March 1977.

Dan's labour would be to Justin's distinct advantage. One day, Dan was duplicating some of his brother's demo tapes when a Rondor employee, David Owen, overheard the music. The result was remarkable for a struggling muso fresh out of college: Owen reportedly secured Justin an £18,000 advance and set him to work creating various jingles for a host of clients.

Through this job, Justin met a man who would be a big part of The Darkness's identity and family. Pedro Ferreira was a Portuguese Black Sabbath fanatic who ran the recording studios where Justin fashioned his jingles. The two became great friends and Ferreira would go on to become The Darkness's sound engineer, producer and the man who carried Justin around on his shoulders come the last song of the live show. He would also earn the nickname 'Pedrock'.

Working to briefs delivered by an advertising agency, Justin would fashion tunes for the likes of Mars bars, Children's Tax Credit, Selfridges, Popstars, Tango and IKEA. In the last case, he successfully composed a tune for an advert that would be considered the third most annoying of 2002 by *Marketing* magazine. 'He seemed quite happy about all his work,' says James Leah. 'After being on the dole, then coming to London and getting a bloody good job, it must have seemed great. He liked doing the keyboard stuff – he did it at home as a hobby, anyway. Here, he was getting paid for it.'

As time would tell, however, Justin Hawkins's talent was destined to achieve far more than shifting fizzy drinks and furniture.

'There was no way in the world I was going to miss being a part of The Darkness'
FRANKIE

*Dan realised that Justin was better than any* **frontman** *he was likely to find*

# Chapter 4
# DARKNESS DESCENDS

**D**an Hawkins couldn't quite believe his eyes. He had always known his brother was a congenital extrovert, but this was astonishing. At midnight, the old millennium would make way for the new, and the Hawkins family had gathered in the Gillingham Swan pub, near the Suffolk town Beccles, to celebrate. 'We were all getting pissed,' Dan would tell *Kerrang!*. 'Justin and I were laughing at our dad dancing.'

Then Justin decided to provoke chuckles himself. Suddenly, he was the centre of attention, dancing in a wildly demonstrative fashion to the schizophrenic peaks and troughs of Queen's epic 1975 operatic rock song 'Bohemian Rhapsody'. 'It was the funniest thing I've ever seen,' recalled Dan. 'I was nodding my head and smiling and rocking. It was the same reaction that people get when they see The Darkness for the first time.'

At that moment, Dan realised that his own brother was better than any frontman he was likely to find.

The Darkness was born at exactly the right time. Even Dan Hawkins's tireless resolve was starting to flag. The previous two years had not seen major career advancements for our cast. Dan and Frankie shared a flat in Shepherd's Bush and formed a band named Empire – an outfit of no fixed stylistic abode, with a singer who apparently sounded something like George Michael. 'I answered an ad that Dan had put in the music press,' Frankie has related. 'We were trying to get something together. But, when Justin came back from college, he wasn't keen on being in a band with Dan.'

Despite initially feeling that he 'couldn't be arsed with the politics' of playing alongside his brother, Justin did eventually join the band, taking an uncharacteristically peripheral role on synthesisers. Then Empire sacked their singer. 'We never really had a proper direction in Empire,' Frankie later conceded. 'Our singer was incredible to start with, but it just didn't work out as we wanted it to, so he had to go.'

After a series of Sunday afternoons spent auditioning hopeful singers, Empire eventually looked within its own ranks. 'Dan suggested that I give it a go,' Justin recalled. 'We had tried so many singers before and even though they had their merits I had this overwhelming feeling that I was better than all of them put together. Despite Justin's adopting the frontman's role with relative ease, the band still failed to gel. 'Justin had a shot at singing,' Frankie recalled, 'but because the music was much more downbeat it didn't really work.'

In the grand scheme of rock, the best thing about Empire was that it piqued Sue Whitehouse's interest. Sue was bookkeeper for the Verve's manager, John Best, who was looking for new talent. Whitehouse convinced him that Empire were worthy of his attention and promptly began managing them. She found them equipment, booked them into London rehearsal studios and started looking for a record deal, which never came.

When interviewed by the *NME* in 2003, John Best couldn't even remember what Empire sounded like. 'They just frittered away my money,' he said with hilarious candour. 'I don't think they were up to much. That bassist was always hanging around the office. He was very tall.'

Following the inevitable collapse of Empire, the very tall Frankie became sick of unemployment. 'My brother was a bit of a beach bum,' he would relate, 'and he worked with this tour company in Venezuela, taking students around the mountains. So I went over to help out.' Dan became a jobbing session guitarist for the likes of Natalie Imbruglia. It may have helped pay the bills, but contributing anonymous guitar licks to other people's albums was clearly not what he had been striving for all those years. 'It wasn't a good time, I must admit,' he later reflected. Ed, by this point, had completed an HND at Salisbury University, before returning to Lowestoft to work at Sanyo. He told Radio 1, 'After studying TV and film, I came home and got my first job in television … on the production line.' He would shortly up sticks to London, joining local rockers Q*Sling.

Justin stayed in London, living in Archway and continuing with his jingle work. Having parted company with Rondor, he was freelancing and would now sing on his compositions, providing his own lyrical slogans. He created a 'sting' for Cartoon Network and music for an award-winning French film, which apparently didn't give him the courtesy of an on-screen credit.

'Some of the songs he did', reckons James Leah, 'were a bit silly. There was one song for Bird's Eye – Eastern Curry or something like that – and he wrote a song for it called "Beast from the East", which he sang in a John Shuttleworth-type Northern voice.

He made loads of pitches to different companies, and didn't get them all – he liked to do things his way. But he did get quite a few commissions.'

Perhaps the most challenging task of Justin's jingle career was set by Yahoo!. For the benefit of an advert, he was told to walk down Oxford Street, singing to people while playing guitar. James Leah recalls, 'The advertising company asked him what he needed, in order to do it, and he said, "I need loads of beer." It was recorded for radio and stressed him out. He got completely pissed before doing it.'

While stunts like this further outlined Justin's capacity for attention-grabbing shenanigans, it presently seemed that his career was going in a very non-rock direction. Yet all this jingle writing arguably honed his songwriting skills and led to the infuriatingly catchy songs that would later infiltrate the Top Forty on a regular basis.

'I'm not ashamed of all that jingle stuff,' Justin would tell the Sun. 'People tell me it's not cool but as far as I'm concerned it's music.'

As usual, Justin couldn't stop himself from dabbling with ideas for several bands at once. He toyed with the idea of starting a pop act called Magnet Watch, whose name was based on the Nintendo 64 console game *Goldeneye*. Then there was E-Wing and the intriguing project Dad. This last one was unsurprisingly set to enlist people's fathers. At one point, there was talk that Justin's practically inclined father might fashion some wooden instruments, specifically for the project.

Yes, with such foolish plans in the air, and Dan's despondency growing, The Darkness was not so much an option as a necessity.

Perhaps driven by a sense of new, postmillennial possibilities, Justin, Dan and Ed started enthusing about this incredible new band they were going to form, making a solemn oath never to give up on it. Justin emailed Frankie in Venezuela, asking him if he wanted to play bass. He soon flew home. 'Too f*****g right I came back straightaway, man!' Frankie would tell *Metal Hammer*. 'There was no way in the world I was going to miss being a part of The Darkness.'

While the press later focused on the band's being named after Ed's dark mood swings, the band would dismiss this as 'a silly in-joke that got out of hand'. Justin would tell *Kerrang!*, 'The truth is that we tried to find the most inappropriate name known to man. And somehow, we've grown into it.'

Once all four members were assembled in the same country, Sue Whitehouse reprised her managerial role, booking the band into an Acton rehearsal room. From the start, it was obvious that something fresh was building between them. Ed would later put it partly down to the unique chemistry between the two seemingly contradictory Hawkins brothers: 'If this was a band with just Justins in it, or just Dans, I don't think I'd want to be in it. There's a balance between them musically that just works.'

One of their earliest creations, the rollicking rocker 'Black Shuck', would kick-start The Darkness's live set for years and eventually opened the *Permission To Land* album. Lyrically steeped in East Anglian folklore, it was

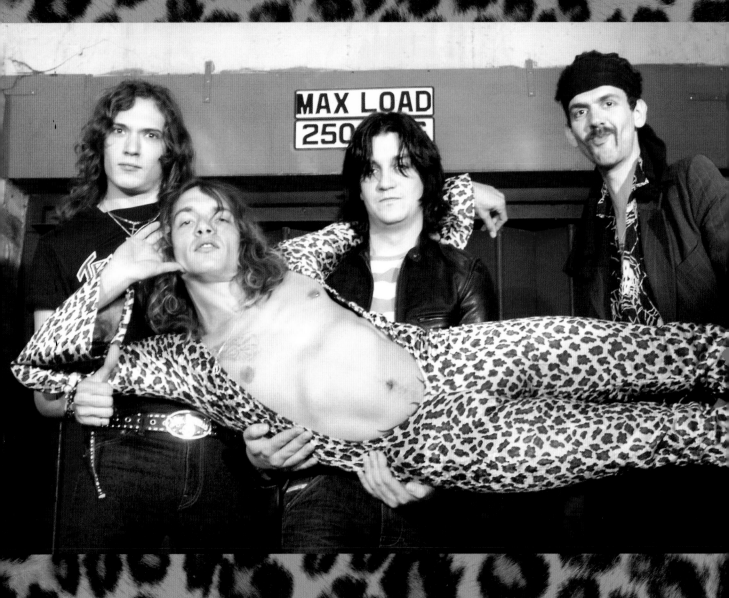

*Justin, Dan and Ed started*
*enthusing about this*
**incredible new band**
*they were going to form*

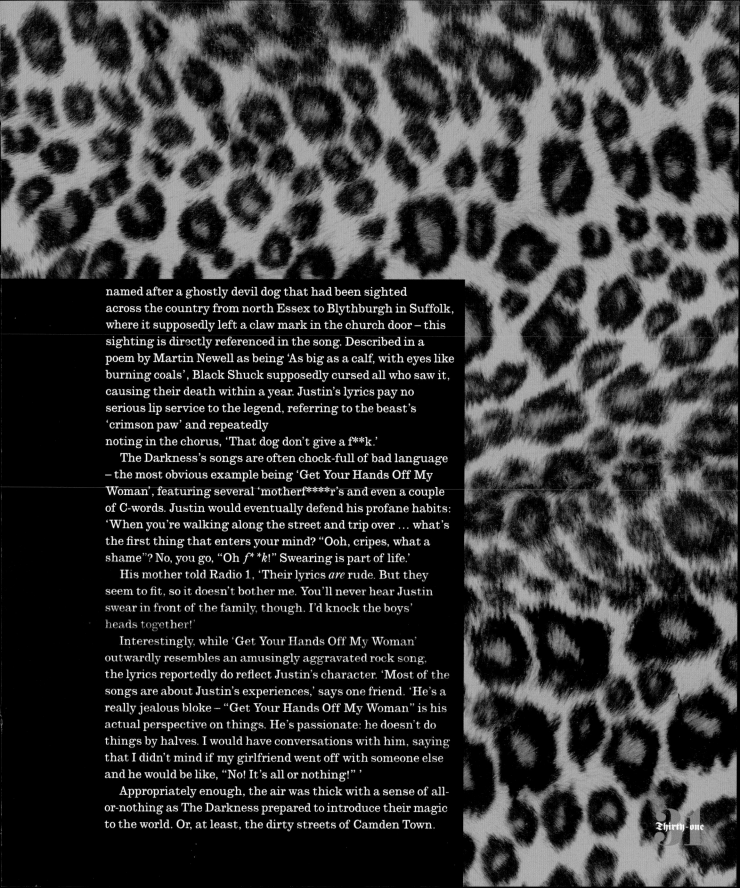

named after a ghostly devil dog that had been sighted
across the country from north Essex to Blythburgh in Suffolk,
where it supposedly left a claw mark in the church door – this
sighting is directly referenced in the song. Described in a
poem by Martin Newell as being 'As big as a calf, with eyes like
burning coals', Black Shuck supposedly cursed all who saw it,
causing their death within a year. Justin's lyrics pay no
serious lip service to the legend, referring to the beast's
'crimson paw' and repeatedly
noting in the chorus, 'That dog don't give a f\*\*k.'

The Darkness's songs are often chock-full of bad language
– the most obvious example being 'Get Your Hands Off My
Woman', featuring several 'motherf\*\*\*\*r's and even a couple
of C-words. Justin would eventually defend his profane habits:
'When you're walking along the street and trip over … what's
the first thing that enters your mind? "Ooh, cripes, what a
shame"? No, you go, "Oh *f\**k!" Swearing is part of life.'

His mother told Radio 1, 'Their lyrics *are* rude. But they
seem to fit, so it doesn't bother me. You'll never hear Justin
swear in front of the family, though. I'd knock the boys'
heads together!'

Interestingly, while 'Get Your Hands Off My Woman'
outwardly resembles an amusingly aggravated rock song,
the lyrics reportedly do reflect Justin's character. 'Most of the
songs are about Justin's experiences,' says one friend. 'He's a
really jealous bloke – "Get Your Hands Off My Woman" is his
actual perspective on things. He's passionate: he doesn't do
things by halves. I would have conversations with him, saying
that I didn't mind if my girlfriend went off with someone else
and he would be like, "No! It's all or nothing!" '

Appropriately enough, the air was thick with a sense of all-
or-nothing as The Darkness prepared to introduce their magic
to the world. Or, at least, the dirty streets of Camden Town.

*Standing atop that counter was one Justin Hawkins, posing as if he were the* **King of England**

# Chapter 5

# SATURDAY NIGHT'S ALRIGHT FOR GURNING

By the year 2000, London's Barfly had long been a venue known for breaking new talent. An unknown Welsh trio called Stereophonics showcased here in the mid-nineties and went on to fill Wembley Arena. Situated above the Monarch pub in the Chalk Farm end of Camden Town, the Barfly comprises a small room with a bar directly facing the stage.

Today was Saturday, 12 August. At this point, Saturday night shows at the Barfly weren't heavily promoted – they were three-band bills of newcomers that casual weekend thrill seekers might fancy checking out. Picture the scene, as a crowd of wide-eyed innocents stared back and forth between the low stage – which held four-fifths of a band, rocking as though their very lives depended on it – and the bar behind them. Standing atop that counter was one Justin Hawkins, posing as if he were the King of England and screaming like a banshee. There was no guitar in his hands at this point – just a microphone. The music was fundamentally traditional rock, yet played with a new, brave energy bordering on fanaticism. This was The Darkness's first London show and the headliners, Lotharian, would have their work cut out for them.

To gain a full understanding of precisely how brave The Darkness were to launch themselves in the year 2000, you need only to glance back at the surrounding musical landscape. In rock the big noise was being made by nu metal, which had been growing exponentially since Korn emerged in 1994. Elsewhere, pop and indie chugged along without much by way of incident. The week that The Darkness played this Barfly show, London also saw dates from Turin Brakes, Coldplay, Badly Drawn Boy, King Adora and Baby Bird. Not a traditional rock band among them. Right now, the music industry placed emphasis on looking to the future. In August 2000, you would have bet good money that The Darkness would be laughed out of the London live scene as quickly as they had arrived.

The Barfly's promoter, Jon McIldowie, initially booked The Darkness on the basis of a three-track CD. Their manager Sue Whitehouse had handwritten 'The Love EP' on the case. Sure enough, the three tracks all concerned affairs of the heart. They were 'I Believe In a Thing Called Love' (a big rocker with killer hooklines), 'Love Is Only a Feeling' (an epic, heartfelt tune, which captured Justin at his most lyrically straight-faced) and 'Love on the Rocks With No Ice' (a behemoth of a track, with positively ear-splitting vocals).

While McIldowie wouldn't actually see the band live for some time, his colleague Be Rozzo did catch them. 'It was great,' Rozzo marvels today. 'We all looked at each other and our jaws dropped. You didn't know whether to laugh hysterically and roll around the floor, or just start climbing over the furniture and play air guitar.'

There are two main differences between The Darkness then and now – besides the absence of Frankie's trademark bandanna. The first is the presence of a second guitarist named Chris McDougal, who didn't last long by all accounts. 'They kicked him out' claims one insider. 'He and Ed lived in Finsbury Park for a while, but by the end they didn't get on.' The band presumably didn't fall out with McDougal too badly, as Dan would later include him in his *Permission To Land* thanks list. Most importantly, Justin picked up the fallen guitar and was one step closer to becoming the rock god we see today.

The other difference back then was the occasional outbreak of blatant humour in the songs themselves. 'Black Shuck' originally began with a Vincent Price-esque spoken-word intro from Justin. In subsequent years, this would be amputated – the song itself was, after all, amusing enough.

'Justin also made a lot more "devil's horns" signs with his fingers,' observes Be Rozzo of the old days, 'between almost every lick on the guitar! The roadie was carting Justin around on his shoulders. They've been doing that for ever – it was comedy stuff. The whole thing was about enjoying yourself for a change.'

One pre-show ritual that has remained constant for The Darkness is the group hug. Before hitting the stage, they will huddle together in rugby scrum formation and whisper to each other. 'It's f*****g important,' Dan later stressed to *Bang* magazine. 'I can't discuss what we talk about [in the hug], but we like to get together to remind ourselves who we are.' Among the expressions overheard by *Word* magazine's Roy Wilkinson, however, were 'Let's make this great!', 'Keep it tight!' and the even more profound 'Let's go and have some f*****g fun!'

Jon McIldowie continued to book The Darkness, he says, 'for two reasons. I liked them and they brought a crowd. In the beginning it was just their mates, then the more gigs they did, people found out about it. After a while they had a cult following of about two hundred. For a lazy promoter, it was a dream.'

'We deliberately played at the weekends,' Frankie has recalled, 'so we wouldn't expose ourselves to the industry, but even then it was sporadic shows that were largely met with derision.'

The Darkness may have been determined to circumvent the industry, but the industry came to them, nevertheless. Says McIldowie, 'Scouts would come down and tell everyone they loved it. The ones with the balls to tell this to their bosses were laughed out of the meeting. That was a recurring theme for a long time.'

*The music
was played with a
**new, brave energy**
bordering on
fanaticism*

Be Rozzo adds, 'There used to be more A&R people coming to see The Darkness than most of the supposed "buzz" bands. But they wouldn't sign them, so it was a hilarious situation. I won't name them, but gangs of my A&R mates would regularly phone up genuinely excited, asking when the band were playing next.' 'In a way we've A&R'd ourselves,' Justin later commented. 'All the bits of input we've had, we've completely ignored … if someone suggested trimming Frankie's moustache, he'd grow it longer. Our motto is, "If it's worth doing, it's worth overdoing".'

James Leah saw his friends on stage as The Darkness for the first time at their second show, again at the London Barfly, on Friday, 13 October 2000. Leah had been in hospital earlier that year, quite ill. 'Justin was the only mate who came to see me in Beccles,' he says. 'That's when you know who your friends are. One of my friends who lived up the road couldn't be bothered to come and see me, but Justin came all the way from London with only thirty quid in his pocket. He played me a song called "Get Well Soon" on my piano.' The Darkness played this very same song for Leah's benefit that night.

Leah seconds the motion that the band used to be more deliberately amusing. 'The early gigs were hilarious – much funnier than they are now,' he says. 'For one thing, Justin had a big gut. He'd pull his T-shirt up and it would wobble about as he sang!' Justin would later confirm this to *Dazed & Confused* magazine, saying, 'I wanted to be like Steven Tyler or [late AC/DC frontman] Bon Scott and then realised I was actually closer to Meat Loaf. Which is the wrong end of rock.' Realising that his ticket to rock stardom would never be punched if he had a paunch, Justin embarked on a diet largely consisting of pilchards and vitamin pills, accompanied by endless sit-ups and 'a huge regime of talking about how little I was drinking'. The results are often on display for the ladies today, and indeed some of the men. Justin also used to sport a pair of NHS-style spectacles, which afforded him a geeky chic not dissimilar to that of Pulp's Jarvis Cocker. These were discarded fairly early in the band's career.

While The Darkness were playing only one show a month at this point, their stone gathered moss. Justin's then girlfriend worked in PR and would send group emails out to her industry contacts, telling them about this must-see band. Word of mouth would do the rest. 'They got tighter and added at least one song every other gig,' recalls James

Leah. 'They were on a creative roll. Justin lost weight. He had some really cool T-shirts made up with a one-eyed Black Shuck on it. They gave away Darkness badges, too.'

There were, of course, dissenters. At the third Barfly show, on Saturday, 18 November, one audience member was heard to yell the delicately composed critique, 'Bell ends!' Leah says, laughing, 'Justin didn't hear it at the time, but found it very funny later on.'

The band stuck to playing the Barfly, Dan has reflected, because it was the only venue which would book them. 'You don't have to go all round the country to get a decent following. If you play one venue again and again then people know where to find you.'

Somewhere along the way, Justin had a tattoo of his own first name inked on his left shoulder – the 's' appearing in the form of a thunderbolt. He explained, 'It was originally one of my T-shirt designs, but was such a hit with the ladies that I [inked it on], perma-style. I would encourage folk to mark their own children in the same way.'

Among the new songs that eventually bubbled to the surface was the excellent 'Givin' Up', a straight-ahead rock song with a classic Rolling Quo riff. While it superficially sounds upbeat, it's actually about the ever-decreasing circles of heroin addiction. James Leah says, 'Justin just likes a drink and has smoked cigarettes since he was a young teenager. He was never into drugs – but someone close to him was, at one point.' On the subject of heroin, Justin would tell *Bang* magazine that he knows somebody 'who has been that way inclined for many a moon ... The only way [to approach the problem] is to see it from their perspective, try to understand and to be funny.'

In *Kerrang!*, he confessed, 'I wouldn't feel comfortable trying to approach the subject in a mature, adult way, or by being cryptic about it.'

Another song that ably demonstrates Justin's talent for hurling red herrings at listeners is 'Growing On Me'. One journalist would describe the song's line, 'I want to touch you but I'm afraid of the consequences', as 'quite simply the best, most fragile lyric you'll hear all year'. He might not have felt quite the same way, had he realised the song is about sexually transmitted disease. Such knowledge sheds new light on lines such as 'Can't get you off my head' and '... you're part of me now, and I've only got myself to blame'. Whether Justin was writing from experience is, of course, best left behind closed drawers.

'*Our motto is,*
*"If it's worth doing,*
*it's worth overdoing"*'

JUSTIN

'It would go one of two ways . . .
either nothing would happen,
or they'd be massive'

# Chapter 6
# LET THEM EAT CAKE

One of The Darkness's first shows of 2001 was effectively a rock'n'-roll funeral. The band appeared alongside numerous other acts at Camden's HQ Club, as a tribute to the Q*Sling bassist Sam Powell, Ed's former bandmate, who committed suicide on 2 February.

Justin's mob continued to play the Barfly and still the A&R folk pussyfooted around them like shy teenagers afraid to chat someone up at a party. Justin would tell *Kerrang!*, 'Some of the record companies that were sniffing around would say stuff like, 'How can I be sure that you're not being ironic? How can I market you?' It's just paranoia and ignorance. This is the entertainment trade, and you need to be entertaining people. If you're not doing that, f**k off and work in a library.'

On 5 May, The Darkness did not disband and seek librarians' jobs. They took the relatively adventurous step of playing a short distance from Camden in Kentish Town, at a slightly larger, but less well-known, venue named the Verge. With a capacity of roughly two hundred people, the Verge boasts an onstage pole, which was of course a red rag-bull interface where Justin Hawkins was concerned. The show was promoted by the band's friend Valerie Gayrimond, who had seen them at the Barfly and considered them, 'amazing. They were nice, intelligent, funny people, and their band actually reflected their personalities. I told lots of my friends to go and see them. Even if you didn't like heavy metal, you couldn't help warming to them and having a good time.'

The Verge show was one of Gayrimond's monthly nights, named 'The Fan Club'. As the event was celebrating its first twelve months in operation, The Darkness and their support band, Dead America (destined to rename themselves The Strings, post-9/11), decided to do something extra special and throw on a finger-food buffet for the packed-in punters. The Darkness provided the savouries, while Dead America handled dessert. 'I think they liked the idea that supplying food was quirky and a bit non-rock 'n' roll,' says Gayrimond, laughing. 'It was the irony of a rock band laying on a buffet! I had to check that it would be OK with the venue's management – and they were fine about it, provided no food was thrown anywhere.'

James Leah remembers the buffet as having been Ed's idea. 'The band spent quite a lot of money on all this food. It was put on a trestle table behind the sound engineer and outside the gents'. There weren't much left at the end of the gig. People were so drunk that they didn't think about all the bacteria that was probably on it.'

'Even if you didn't like heavy metal,
you couldn't help warming
to them and having a
good time'

The Darkness even wrote an impromptu tune in the buffet's honour. 'We had a song that listed all the food,' Frankie would fondly recount, 'over a Zeppelin-type riff. We'd go, "Sushi!", then crack into a little Chinese motif.' Justin added, 'Which demonstrated our complete ignorance.' Another seemingly deliberate attempt to get the audience guffawing was a ballad entitled 'Love You Five Times'. 'People loved it as a singalong, but I think Dan maybe vetoed it after a while, in case people didn't take them seriously enough.' A song entitled 'Hell's Gazelle' was also abandoned, when the band realised the feeble nature of the eponymous antelope.

Among the revellers at the Verge was Simon Price, a writer from the *Independent*, whom Gayrimond had enthusiastically persuaded to come down. Initially reluctant due to the band's 'dodgy, gothic-sounding name' and then suitably blown away by The Darkness's performance, Price would pen their first national live review, describing them as 'a histrionic, high camp heavy metal band, best described as a gay AC/DC fronted by a young Freddie Mercury … hugely entertaining, regardless of their exact location on the irony-seriousness scale'. Referring to the 'gay AC/DC' part of that write-up, the band would quip that they'd sooner be considered the straight Queen.

The Darkness played the Verge for the second time on 6 October that year. One unforgettable tale relates how Dan cut his finger quite badly, while hacking cheese into cubes fit for cocktail sticks.

Not all of The Darkness were positive that this was a good idea. This evening, on Friday 16 November 2001, they were unpacking their equipment outside the Castle in Tooting High Street. 'I think we're playing a wedding reception,' said Dan, peering through into a function room where the band had been told to set up.

This was, in fact, a regular night titled 'Rock Apocalypse', attended by those who liked their music hard and heavy. 'The people there that night were rugged-looking, but friendly,' recalls a Castle barman. 'The landlord was strict about fighting – anyone causing trouble was banned.'

The Darkness didn't know this at the time. Which makes it all the more frightening that Justin Hawkins chose tonight to unveil his distinctly feminine, skin-tight catsuit – white, with red thunderbolts down the side and flared trousers. 'I remembered my mum telling me about being in this club and Brian Jones turning up in this pink catsuit … I thought, F**k it! Catsuits are rock 'n' roll. The old feminine/masculine bullshit.'

The frontman located a dancewear company that made Lycra and the rest is history. 'When Justin came out in that catsuit,' says the Castle barman, 'I think it blew the crowd's minds a little bit.'

Those first suits were a bit flimsy,' Justin would admit, 'but I've still got them. I get told off a lot by management for wearing them because you can see ... stuff.' The delicate nature of Justin's apparel would later see him come a cropper when the band played a Welsh kids' TV show one Saturday morning. As Justin performed one of his trademark headstands in a catsuit, the crotch tore open and, as his own mother later phrased it during an interview, 'one of his bollocks fell out'. Justin later laughed, 'That'll end up on *TV's Naughtiest Blunders*. I won't be letting that happen again.'

Despite the seemingly inappropriate nature of the Castle for The Darkness and the poor turn-out, James Leah recalls the show as 'brilliant. Justin had his T-shirt and trousers over the top of his catsuit. He got the shirt off, but the trousers wouldn't go, because he was wearing trainers. So he was struggling on the floor, trying to get them off, while still playing. In the end, me and Greg Moore had to give him a hand.'

Of further entertaining merit were Justin's impressive leaps into midair and an attempt to get the sparse audience clapping along. Incredibly, MTV were recording that night's show and interviewed the band afterwards.

The catsuit has certainly become part and parcel of Justin's Darkness identity, augmenting both the band's glamorous and homophobe-repelling qualities. As 2002 beckoned, the rock star that had always lurked inside the elder Hawkins brother began to break through, as all thoughts of easy-listening music, midi sequencers and indeed jingles were tossed to the seven winds.

While an endless procession of future commentators would contend that there was nothing original about The Darkness, they were somehow forgetting Justin Hawkins. While the man derived some of his larger-than-life persona and athletics from the ex-Van Halen frontman David Lee Roth and his impish guitar-bashing from the AC/DC guitarist Angus Young, his like had not been seen in rock 'n' roll before. It's all too easy to underestimate not only the skill behind his vocals, but their unique tone. Admirably avoiding a fake American cadence, Justin's voice isn't purely remarkable for its high range: his regularly pitched singing is equally distinctive. Throw in his utter lack of self-consciousness when it came to stage work and photo sessions, along with the kind of quick-witted interview responses that other frontmen would give their funny bones for, and you have an incredibly fresh, commanding presence.

Thankfully, no one else in The Darkness showed even vague signs of discontentment that Justin increasingly became the focus of attention. As Dan would tell *Metal Hammer*, 'If you have a star as a frontman who simply doesn't give a flying f**k and you never know what he's going to get up to onstage every night, that takes the pressure off.'

Justin and his bandmates had reverted to their old habit of playing Sunday football. This time, they were playing in a team called the Angels, alongside and against other music-industry types who would congregate in Regent's Park for a good, healthy kickabout. The Barfly promoter Jon McIldowie was on their side and came to know the boys well. 'They were good footballers,' he reports, 'apart from Ed, who just came and watched and drank. We had a goalkeeper called the Shadow, who worked for [the record company] Food at the time.' It comes as no surprise to hear which position Justin adopted in the team. 'He was the centre forward – he was always at the front trying to score the goals and take all the glory.'

Without consciously trying to advance themselves in the industry, The Darkness met a lot of lawyers and record-company folk through these sessions. These people would come to know them on a social level, before they even knew about the band. It certainly couldn't, and wouldn't, do them any harm.

Having by now seen The Darkness perform, McIldowie was aware of the band's full potential. He reasoned that their extreme nature could only provoke extreme reactions. 'I thought it would go one of two ways,' he says. 'Either nothing would happen or they'd be massive. I sent an email to a lawyer friend in December 2001 and told him about them. He had been asking for music industry tips, but didn't follow mine up.' That's yet another industry figure who'll be kicking himself today.

As Christmas beckoned, The Darkness could rest up, content in the knowledge that the New Year would see their first trip to America.

*The catsuit* has become part and parcel of Justin's *Darkness identity*

## Chapter 7
# THE TEXAS CATSUIT MASSACRE

**A**ustin, Texas, would be the location of The Darkness's most intrepid venture yet – an appearance at the South by Southwest event. Established in 1987, it is part festival, part music-business conference. Each March, music lovers and industry types descend on Austin, securing themselves a badge or wristband, which allows them to see around one thousand bands play in around fifty different venues, over four nights. In November 2001, The Darkness had dispatched a demo to the organisers, along with the $20 registration fee. An enthusiastic email soon came whizzing back across the Atlantic, concluding: 'This shit is immortal! Rock the f**k on!'

Justin recalled, 'They said that out of the thousands of demos they'd received it was the best one. That was pretty refreshing – especially when they invited us over.'

The man responsible for 'Rock the f**k on!' was Craig Stewart, one of South by Southwest's music co-ordinators. Come November each year, he and his colleagues would scan through piles of demo material, looking for bands suitable to play. Coming across The Darkness's CD, which bore the legend 'Songs with love in the title', Stewart spun it and adored it, even though that kind of rock wasn't normally his bag. 'It was like absolutely nothing else,' he says. 'It had its balls on the chopping block. I misread a quote in the press kit – something about their being the gay AC/DC, perhaps. Before I'd even seen a photo, I thought, Oh, that makes it even cooler. That's their shtick – Justin's queer. But I was mistaken!'

After taking the disc home, Stewart played it for his friend John Darnielle, who was in town with his band the Mountain Goats. It was Darnielle, in case you were wondering, who contributed the 'This shit is immortal!' line to that email, while Stewart owns up to the 'Rock the f**k on!'.

The band promptly organised and paid for their trip. 'We'd go out of business very quickly if we paid for accommodations and travel,' notes Stewart. 'They definitely spent a lot of money to get here. I even hinted to Sue that they might be expecting too much from our forty-minute set, when there's so much competition at the event. But they were really enthusiastic about it.'

Arriving a couple of days before their 15 March show, The Darkness met up with Craig Stewart, who thought them, 'totally sweet and dead cool'. Then they went to check out the venue. A two-hundred-capacity club on Austin's central Sixth Street, Maggie Mae's had a tiny stage positioned in the middle of the floor. Shaking off their horror, the band made the best of things as ever and populated the stage with whatever equipment they could squeeze on. On the night, they played to 75 people – a turnout with which Stewart was 'pleasantly surprised. They were definitely cramped on stage, but they made it work. Justin was all over the low stage and went out in the audience a little bit. There was microphone twirling. It was fabulous.' He adds that spectators seemed impressed. 'Everyone who was there pretty much loved them. They're undeniable – when you see them live, what kind of person could not like that?'

Before heading back across the Pond, The Darkness played their second US show, at the traditional glam-rock haven the Roxy on Los Angeles' guitar-friendly Sunset Strip. Behind the scenes, however, the band had experienced a shock wave. Dan, Ed and Frankie discovered that Justin and their manager Sue had secretly been an item for some time now. Before being found out, the couple had intended to get married and really surprise everyone.

Justin would be quoted as saying in the Sun, 'Sue went to a management seminar and the first thing they said was, "You can't have a relationship with a member of the band." It's going to be difficult but we're getting through it …' He added, 'We wondered if people would approve of us going out, because she's been managing us for so long. It was like we were having an illicit affair but it was just two people getting together.'

Their revelation temporarily shook The Darkness – no doubt because of worries about how this might affect the band's future. Frankie later admitted that emotions ran high: 'Lots of stuff was said that shouldn't have been … You get really paranoid at moments like that. Are Sue and Justin just going to do their own thing? Is Justin going to go solo?'

Justin felt his bandmates were 'being quite immature' about the situation. He would tell *The Face*, 'They wanted to sack Sue. I said, "If you sack her, you sack me". When they realised I owned all the guitars and the amps, they realised they couldn't do f**k all about it.'

While Justin later remarked that the near-split had destroyed his faith in humanity, the dust outwardly settled. He bought Sue an engagement ring and the happy couple became common-law man and wife. This effectively made Justin stepfather to Sue's daughter Charlotte. 'Justin's much more confident now and far more grown up than he was,' believes his friend James Leah. 'Becoming a stepfather to Sue's child has made him a lot more serious. He's even a bit more serious on stage – maybe he's become more conscious of his age, like everyone does.'

Upon returning to Britain, The Darkness strapped on their blagging hats and approached various music equipment companies in an attempt to prise free gear out of them. Legend has it that Justin secured a Mesa/Boogie endorsement by ringing the company up and playing a guitar solo down the phone line.

For one night only in April, The Darkness underwent a sudden and dramatic change of image. Sue acted on a *Music Week* advert placed by a stylist, who specialised in theatrical costume. The idea was to experiment with a new look for the band and things initially appeared promising.

'When we met her it was unbelievable,' Dan told the style mag *Dazed & Confused*. 'We were all totally sucked into her world. She claimed to have styled the royal family of Luxembourg.'

The stylist's visions came to life during the band's 5 April show at Hackney's Ocean 2 venue. Justin appeared on stage in an outfit involving fluffy lion trousers and a foxtail belt. Dan had been cast as a wizard, modelling a cloak with owl feathers around the collar, making for a Henry VIII-esque effect. Frankie sported a dandy Edwardian jacket with snakes sewn into the lapels, while the relatively fortunate Ed was kitted out with a Flash Gordon-style black sleeveless shirt and nifty shoulder pads.

Inevitably, this arrangement was doomed. Even more inevitably, Justin was the only one who became attached to at least half of his new kit – he continued wearing the fluffy trousers for some time.

Another significant date on The Darkness's calendar was 11 June, when they played Wolverhampton Varsity. This might have been a dismal out-of-town Tuesday night show, had it not been for the fact that the band were being trailed by a journalist and photographer from *Dazed & Confused*. The resultant ten-page feature – accompanied by the cover lines NO LABEL. NO HYPE. WHY THE DARKNESS ROCK and lush photography that sold the band as true stars – followed them up the motorway in their archetypal clapped-out VW camper van. Five people then watched the band play: the *Dazed & Confused* duo, manager Sue and her brother, plus a local sound man.

At one point during the show, Justin made perhaps his most ingenious utterance in the band's history. 'I dedicate the next song to you five,' he declared. 'You know who you are'. Then Frankie answered his chiming mobile phone, only to find his mother on the line. All of which was a journalist's wet dream.

The next day before their show at Oxford Street's Metro venue, Dan told the *Dazed* writer, 'If we end up playing on the pub circuit and making a living from that in ten to fifteen years' time then that's just the way it has to be.' Just over a year later, Justin found himself talking to *Kerrang!* about that very article. 'The whole point of the feature was, "Don't forget there are people like these, who will probably never make it, but that's not gonna stop 'em from toiling."' Given that Justin was having his picture taken for the cover of *Kerrang!* at the time, with a summer of major UK festival appearances ahead of him, that quote was doubtless accompanied by a wry smile.

James Leah next saw the band at London's Camden Underworld on 9 August. He was taken aback by the extent of their development. 'They'd changed completely,' he recounts. 'They went from being comedic and funny, to being quite serious. It looked like they were more professional. They were more aware of their appearance, and how they appeared to other people. They were more audience-aware and had been thinking about it more. Also, the songs were a lot tighter. You'd could hear that they'd been practising a lot, honing the songs.'

By this point, The Darkness looked as if they knew they were rock stars. 'I went backstage and it was really quiet,' says Leah. 'They weren't joking about any more. They were really focused and not so easy to have conversations with. It felt like a whole different playing field. Yet I still didn't recognise that they were gonna be megastars at all.'

Around that period, Justin spoke to one friend about the depth of his ambition for the first time. 'I asked Justin what would happen if they didn't get signed. He said he'd go into doing music and film scores, but added that it wouldn't get him on the front of magazines. That's when I realised he really wanted to be famous. At that point, it all seemed like an obtainable objective. It was like he'd taken a big leap of confidence.'

Three days after the Underworld show, the band's debut single emerged through the minuscule UK label Must Destroy. Established by the Notting Hill club DJs Ian Johnsen and Alan Hake, the label had previously handled the odd small-scale release such as an International Noise Conspiracy seven-inch. Yet, having seen The Darkness raze the Barfly, they knew they had to play some part in unleashing them upon the cosmos. Johnsen said, 'Me and my girlfriend stood with our jaws on the floor. We couldn't stop talking about them afterwards.'

One day in the summer of 2002, Sue Whitehouse phoned Johnsen. 'She asked if we wanted to put a single out. I said, "Surely you've been signed by now!" but she said, "No. Everyone's seen us and everyone says the same thing. They like it but they don't know what to do with it." Well, we didn't care about all that – we just wanted to have a f*****g great record out on our label.'

That, they ably achieved. With a strikingly sleazy cover photograph of the band surrounded by rock-'n'-roll paraphernalia, the CD featured the three songs that had appeared on the 'Love' demo, with 'I Believe In a Thing Called Love' as the lead track. The Radio 1 DJs Jo Whiley and Zoe Ball picked up on the band and started spinning the single. Speaking to *Kerrang!*, Whiley later went so far as to publicly defend them. 'We're such boring stiffs in this country,' she said. 'We don't know how to handle showmanship. I love all that stuff and The Darkness do it so well. It's a shame that people have to be cynical about it.'

For every one cynic, however, there seemed to be a few music fans with their ears pricking up. The initial two thousand copies of 'I Believe In a Thing Called Love' sold out swiftly, reaching 180 in the UK charts. Justin would make a point of reading that number out on stage, in the style of a Northern darts commentator. More pressings of the single followed, and these got higher into the charts each time. The disc generally received good reviews, with *Kerrang!* in particular picking up on the band. One writer at the *NME*, on the other hand, had suggested that The Darkness should be killed, which unsurprisingly soured relations between magazine and band from the off. 'That review was very much playing along with the band,' offered *NME*'s editor, Conor McNicholas, in 2003, 'but perhaps it wasn't the most complimentary thing ever written in the paper.'

Justin has generally maintained good humour in the face of criticism. He told Radio 1, 'If you don't think this is a great band, I'm going to walk away from you … if you pursue me [I'll] say, "Please stop following me. You're starting to freak me out."'

*By this point, The Darkness looked as if they knew they were were rock stars*

Come mid-September, The Darkness gained more attention by winning the New Bands competition at Manchester's annual In the City event. Despite this victory, The Darkness became the first band in years not to land a record deal as a result.

On 25 September, they played an event at London's small-scale King's Cross Water Rats club, under the banner 'Best of In The City Unsigned'. Turning in another electrifying performance, they garnered a top-honours five-K live review from *Kerrang!*. Struck by the band's 'air of flamboyant otherness', Dave Everley described them as 'the most talked-about band in Britain' and rightly pointed out that 'in Justin Hawkins's head this tiny bar in London's seediest area is Wembley Stadium, Madison Square Garden and the Budokan rolled into one'.

That night, Justin demonstrated his ability to hand journalists quotes on a silver platter. As Everley entered the band's cramped dressing room, containing 'friends, fans and total strangers', Hawkins looked over and said, 'Sorry, we're all out of cocaine and girls.'

Splendid work. Today, King's Cross. Tomorrow – another show.

*By now, Justin was often* **holding up his thumbs** *during live shows — a gesture that proved infectious*

# Chapter 8
# NO TURNING BACK

Whereas other unsigned bands might sit around waiting for a big record company to sign them and hand over cash for them to make an album, The Darkness were way more proactive. They decided to make the album and then see who wanted to release it. Justin would tell the *Sun* that he financed the album with £20,000 of his own money, accrued from his jingle career. 'IKEA paid for the making of *Permission To Land*,' he said. 'In many ways, it's a flat-pack album.'

As autumn 2002 gave way to winter, The Darkness settled down with their producer pal Pedro Ferreira for three weeks of intensive preproduction work. This involved going through the songs chord by chord, changing the arrangements and fine-tuning the odd tempo. The album itself was then recorded in two weeks at Lincolnshire's Chapel Studios. 'My favourite albums are recorded as quickly as possible,' Justin explained to the *Independent*, 'so you get a chronological indication of where the band were at, at that particular moment.'

'We worked really hard on it,' Dan told dotmusic.com, 'We averaged about two hours' sleep a night when recording because we did it all live.'

Another reason for the quick recording of the actual album was almost certainly the band's low tolerance for repetition. One friend who visited the studio for a day reports that the members 'seemed bored out of their skulls. Justin prefers performing, but because he's so creative he also likes coming up with the songs. I don't think he's keen on redoing the same thing over and over again in the studio.'

One of the last additions to the album was 'Friday Night'. Lyrically the most British of tunes, it was the sound of US rockers Cheap Trick writing music with the Cure, then enlisting Pulp's Jarvis Cocker to write some warmly nostalgic words. While recalling an old flame at school, Justin lists his weekly activities at the time, including badminton, archery and – wait for it – needlework. Not 'particularly cool', as the song itself confesses, but the net result is sublime pop-rock.

Justin claimed that he wanted to call the record *Death In Both Ears*, *Women Who Exaggerate* or the especially ticklesome *Thank You, This Will Suffice For Me, Now If You Please Some Sex For My Friends*. Many more bogus titles would spontaneously dribble from the man's irrepressible mouth, right up until the announcement of the real one, *Permission To Land*. By the time he started claiming that the album would answer to the name *Short Fat Cock*, however, he was patently fooling no one.

That Christmas, The Darkness's Lowestoft natives went home and caught up with some friends in their old haunt, Forbes Brewery, which was now renamed Green Jack. 'They were talking about their band taking off,' recalls their school friend John King. 'A lot of people in the pub seemed really pleased for them. They said that more people might hear about them in February, because they had another single coming out. Now, of course, it's snowballed. Seeing them on MTV blows my mind.'

In January 2003, Justin, Sue and her daughter Charlotte sat in the West Hampstead branch of Pizza Express, taking a moment to enjoy the calm before the storm that this year would inevitably bring. As Justin would note, they had pushed the rock to the top of the hill and given it a shove. Now it was just a matter of keeping up with it.

James Leah, who was also present at Pizza Express, had started to grasp the enormity of what was happening to his old friend. 'Justin told me that Guns N' Roses wanted The Darkness to support them, but their management didn't. I thought he was taking the piss, but he was serious. That's when I knew they were going to make it.'

According to Leah, Justin neither seemed worried about the speed at which things were moving, nor bragged about his achievements. 'He's never been a boaster – he's just had a quiet confidence. Whenever he's excited, he normally calls me, but modestly mentions stuff in passing. We'd be talking about everyday stuff, then he'd casually mention that they were playing with Def Leppard.'

Indeed, The Darkness were, over the course of a nine-date UK trek that would teach them several things. Lesson One: avoid accidents. Justin learned this during the tour's first three shows, which saw him punching through ceilings, splitting his lips inside and out and breaking a toe while smashing a dressing room chair. Lesson Two involved the trashing of dressing rooms. As Justin would recall during a web chat via the *Sun*'s site, 'A lot of these things backfire on us quite badly. We trashed a dressing room at the Sheffield Arena, and the next day Leppard put us in an electrical cupboard.' Frankie discovered Lesson Three after telling Def Leppard's tour manager that the catering was worse than prison food. The rest of the tour saw them being offered a choice of cheese or ham sandwiches with no butter.

Perhaps the most important thing The Darkness learned during these dates was to be themselves, no matter what the adversity. 'That's where we really learned how to be a support band,' recalled Justin, 'which meant doing what you do with no apologies whatsoever.'

'They made me smile,' Def Leppard's singer Joe Elliot told *The Face*. Every note they play I can tell you which Thin Lizzy album it came off, which Rainbow album it came off, which AC/DC album it came off.'

'Def Leppard came in to see us with a bottle of champers,' Frankie informed the BBC, 'and said, "When we started the band we put you in a bottle and we opened it last year. Playing with you is like being sixteen again."'

By now, Justin was often holding up his thumbs during live shows – a gesture that proved infectious. 'Rather than getting people to clap,' he explained, 'we

*They had pushed the rock to the top of the hill and given it a shove.*

ask them to get their thumbs out – or thumb, if they're holding a drink.' Justin's mother would shed light on the growing thumb cult when she spoke to Radio 1: 'Every time the camera came out in our family ... Justin would push his way into every photograph, even if it was of the dog or the hamster. And he would always have his thumb up!'

Most rock fans raised their thumbs for The Darkness's second single, 'Get Your Hands Off My Woman', the 24 February release of which was nicely framed by the last few Leppard dates. A brave choice of single, given the foul nature of its mouth, the song nevertheless infiltrated the UK charts at Number 43, was hailed as *Kerrang!*'s Single of the Week and picked up a Golden God award from *Metal Hammer*. As Justin would rhetorically ask, 'How many unsigned bands have made it into the charts with a song that features the word "c**t" twice and "motherf****r" eight times?' In truth, the band did record a radio edit for the song, which saw those offending words replaced by 'coconut' and 'mother father' respectively. 'It scans well,' he told one journalist, 'so we're all right.'

On 14 March, The Darkness made their second appearance at South by Southwest. As they still weren't earning much at this point, Dan sold his record collection in order to pay for his flight. This time the band played to around 350 people at a show mounted by the British Phonographic Industry, which was naturally intended to promote homegrown rock. Despite playing below their fellow countrymen 80s Matchbox B-Line Disaster on the bill, The Darkness naturally didn't *behave* like supports. 'To me they seemed like the headliners,' says South by Southwest's Craig Stewart. 'There were heaps of people there for them and, maybe because it was a bigger stage, the whole thing seemed even more bombastic than before.'

'Rock isn't a joke in America,' said Dan. 'Just like no one went to see Def Leppard for ironic reasons, that crowd were there because they genuinely loved rock. That's why we felt at home.'

This time, the endorphin rush of playing Stateside wasn't tempered by the reality check of playing to five people back in Britain. The band kicked off their first proper UK headline tour on 26 March. Every once in a while, there would be a sign that something special was happening. At the Brighton show on 31 March, one woman ushered her ten-year-old son over to meet the boys. It transpired that this was his first concert. She told them, 'I wanted you to pop his rock cherry – you're the best men for the job!'

Incredibly for a band who were essentially unsigned – still releasing their singles via Must Destroy – this tour ended at the two-thousand-capacity London Astoria, which had been upgraded from the theatre's smaller sister venue, the Mean Fiddler.

The Darkness's conspicuous lack of a record deal continued to beggar belief. Barfly's promoter Be Rozzo marvels, 'The venues they were playing were getting bigger and bigger, and still no big record labels were stepping up to the plate. I know the band were starting to think the whole thing was a joke. They still didn't have the deal in place. How many more people did they

have to put in a room before someone said, "All right – let's sign the band"?'

The answer came shortly. On 12 May, after much behind-the-scenes deal shaping, The Darkness finally signed to EastWest Records, which meant their records would be released through the colossal Atlantic in America. Inevitably, the band made even signing their contract a source of entertainment. Dressed as eighteenth-century noblemen, they used quills to scribble their names and brandished a comedy cheque made out for 'Three pints of lager and a vodka, lime and soda'. If you examined it closely, you would see that the cheque had been drawn from the Rock Bank and was numbered 666.

The Darkness had taken almost two years to achieve all this, but the corporate muscle and expectations of a major record label would now elevate them to a whole new level, in one fell swoop. Thankfully, being level-headed characters, the band knew it. Ed's flatmate Greg Moore recalls going out for a few drinks with the drummer around this whole period. 'He told me it was going to get really crazy,' recalls Moore, 'and that life would really change for him. And he was completely right.'

At the start of the year, Justin had told *Classic Rock* magazine, 'I have an evil plot where I'll go from being an unknown no-hoper to an evil genius and that'll be it – no in-between. It'll be overnight. I'll wake up one morning, and there you go.'

He was perhaps half-joking. Yet that morning was just around the corner.

*Being taken seriously has been one of The Darkness's* ***greatest battles***

# Chapter 9
# SPINAL TRAP

Towards Christmas 1996 at Huddersfield Technical College, music-technology students were afforded a treat by Sarah Hutton, a lecturer who specialises in the music business. She played them a video of Rob Reiner's classic spoof 'rockumentary' *This Is Spinal Tap*. Centring on a gormless rock band and their baseball-bat-wielding manager, whose cliché-riddled antics were loosely based on the likes of Led Zeppelin, the 1984 movie is a deathless guide to rock 'n' roll's most buffoonish extremities.

'There's a lot to be learned from it,' says Hutton today. 'How not to be a dorky band, for starters. It also showcases some classic gigging problems, such as getting lost between the dressing room and the stage. Every gigging band has a Spinal Tap moment.' It's unclear whether Justin actually watched the film at Huddersfield, but he had doubtless seen it before. Many of his intentionally funny interview quotes in subsequent years might as well have been plucked directly from its script.

Spinal Tap, along with Justin's razor-sharp sense of humour, would prove a curse and a blessing for The Darkness. For a classic-rock-style band to hit the modern-day music scene with straight faces, things would have been difficult enough. But a classic-rock-style band with an often hilarious frontman were wide open to criticism that they were playing it for laughs.

Many folk simply couldn't believe the band's cheek. In June 2003, Justin told *Kerrang!*, 'We get guys in bands telling us what we do is kind of what they do at the end of their session when they're just pissing around, having a great time. They wish, in some ways, that they had the balls to come and do what we do. Because the riffs we play are the sort that make your balls feel big – the kind of stuff you long to be able to get away with.'

Some, however, believed that The Darkness *shouldn't* be getting away with it. One of their most surprising critics has been Motörhead's leader Lemmy Kilminster. 'The Darkness are a novelty group, a cabaret act,' he told *The Face*. 'They should be on at the Wigan Casino.' The basis of Lemmy's condemnation was unclear: maybe he felt the band hadn't paid their dues, or saw them as lampooning rock 'n' roll. The fact remained that he was speaking for a portion of music fans. Being taken seriously has been one of The Darkness's greatest battles.

During 2003 in particular, journalists would queue to ask the band whether they were being ironic. In February, Justin told the *Guardian*, 'What we do is

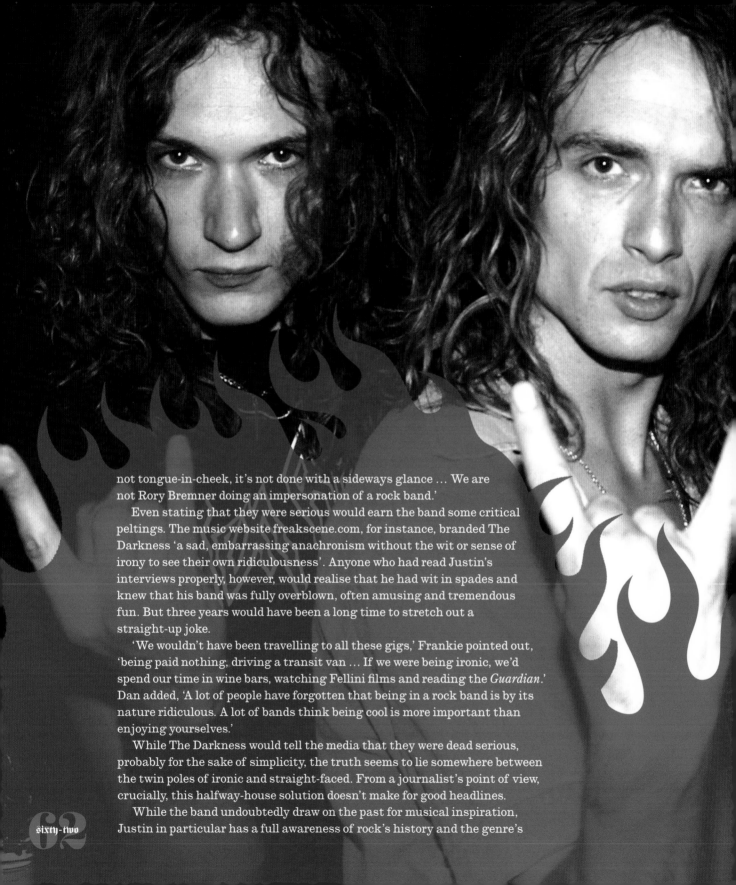

not tongue-in-cheek, it's not done with a sideways glance … We are not Rory Bremner doing an impersonation of a rock band.'

Even stating that they were serious would earn the band some critical peltings. The music website freakscene.com, for instance, branded The Darkness 'a sad, embarrassing anachronism without the wit or sense of irony to see their own ridiculousness'. Anyone who had read Justin's interviews properly, however, would realise that he had wit in spades and knew that his band was fully overblown, often amusing and tremendous fun. But three years would have been a long time to stretch out a straight-up joke.

'We wouldn't have been travelling to all these gigs,' Frankie pointed out, 'being paid nothing, driving a transit van … If we were being ironic, we'd spend our time in wine bars, watching Fellini films and reading the *Guardian*.' Dan added, 'A lot of people have forgotten that being in a rock band is by its nature ridiculous. A lot of bands think being cool is more important than enjoying yourselves.'

While The Darkness would tell the media that they were dead serious, probably for the sake of simplicity, the truth seems to lie somewhere between the twin poles of ironic and straight-faced. From a journalist's point of view, crucially, this halfway-house solution doesn't make for good headlines.

While the band undoubtedly draw on the past for musical inspiration, Justin in particular has a full awareness of rock's history and the genre's

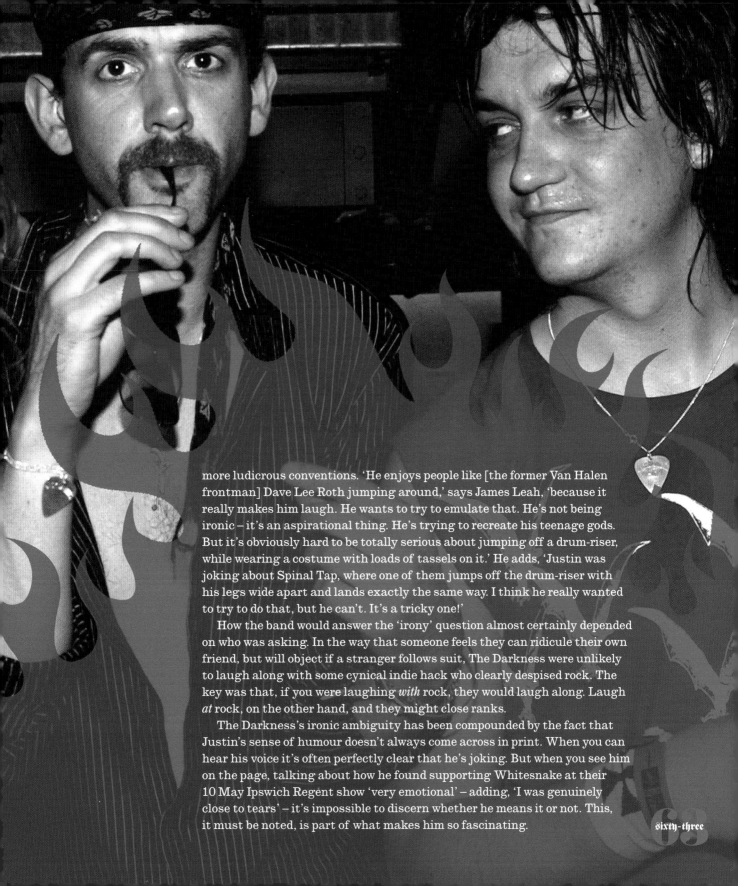

more ludicrous conventions. 'He enjoys people like [the former Van Halen frontman] Dave Lee Roth jumping around,' says James Leah, 'because it really makes him laugh. He wants to try to emulate that. He's not being ironic – it's an aspirational thing. He's trying to recreate his teenage gods. But it's obviously hard to be totally serious about jumping off a drum-riser, while wearing a costume with loads of tassels on it.' He adds, 'Justin was joking about Spinal Tap, where one of them jumps off the drum-riser with his legs wide apart and lands exactly the same way. I think he really wanted to try to do that, but he can't. It's a tricky one!'

How the band would answer the 'irony' question almost certainly depended on who was asking. In the way that someone feels they can ridicule their own friend, but will object if a stranger follows suit, The Darkness were unlikely to laugh along with some cynical indie hack who clearly despised rock. The key was that, if you were laughing *with* rock, they would laugh along. Laugh *at* rock, on the other hand, and they might close ranks.

The Darkness's ironic ambiguity has been compounded by the fact that Justin's sense of humour doesn't always come across in print. When you can hear his voice it's often perfectly clear that he's joking. But when you see him on the page, talking about how he found supporting Whitesnake at their 10 May Ipswich Regent show 'very emotional' – adding, 'I was genuinely close to tears' – it's impossible to discern whether he means it or not. This, it must be noted, is part of what makes him so fascinating.

'Gimme a "D", …
Gimme an "arkness"'

'Musically, the band were taking themselves seriously,' says Valerie Gayrimond of their shows at the Verge, 'but they could see what was funny about all the rock 'n' roll clichés. Just because something's funny, doesn't mean it has to be stupid and ridiculous. Now they're famous, people don't really question it: they either like the band or they don't.'

South by Southwest's Craig Stewart similarly recognises the band's ability to polarise opinion. 'I've figured out that some people hate The Darkness intensely. It's totally black and white. People who don't like them are really resentful about them supposedly being a joke band. I don't really wanna know the answer – either way they're completely brilliant. I don't think they should even answer those questions – they should stay a mystery.'

*Rock Sound* writer Trevor Baker hit the nail on the head when he wrote, 'It's doubtful whether it's even possible to play this kind of heroically ludicrous, madly overblown rock ironically … To rock is a physical thing. It's like asking whether you can have sex ironically.'

Some rock fans were suspicious about the band, from the moment they appeared in that epic *Dazed & Confused* feature. In the last few years, rock has become much more fashionable than it was in the nineties, as the T-shirts of celebrities such as David Beckham will attest, plus celebrities such as Donatella Versace singing The Darkness's praises. Justin expressed bemusement to the *Guardian* about 'models walking around with AC/DC on their arses. If you go to an AC/DC show, you don't see any models. It's mostly men. And the rest of them used to be men.'

The Darkness have shown appreciation that rock's current high profile has helped elevate them. Yet, time and time again, they stress that they neither rely on this nor fear the future. 'We weren't hyped for the first three years and we're still here,' Justin has said. 'We were around before we were fashionable; we are around while we are fashionable; and we'll still be around when we're not fashionable.'

Likewise, the idea of being cool didn't sit easily with the frontman. 'We're still the biggest twats you are likely to encounter, but for some reason that's all the rage now. Being uncool is the new cool.'

Entertainingly, The Darkness have shown little sign of caring whether people understand or even like them. Fashion has shifted around them – not the other way around. After years of being rank outsiders, they still flaunt their underdog spirit with pride. 'We are here to annoy people,' Frankie told the *Guardian* during 2003. 'Just when you think we're gone, we are going to be there, up your arse.'

The bassist's prophecy would be fulfilled. As Britain began to feel the intense summer heat, The Darkness were practically as ubiquitous. On 1 June they played the Download Festival at legendary metal stomping ground Donington Park, in front of thousands of people generally tuned in to the heavier side of things. Remembering lessons learned on the Def Leppard tour, the band pressed on and stormed it, with only a few bruises from projectiles to complain about. They approached the Full Force Festival in Leipzig, Germany, in exactly the same way. 'The weather was miserable and the bill was mostly full of violent, scowling rap-rock bands,' recalled Justin. 'I said to the organiser, "We must be the gayest band on the bill." He said, "Yes, and you would also be the gayest band if you were playing next to the Village People." We went out there, costume changes, no apologies and rocking to the maximum. They loved us because, by that point, we were not slightly apologetic about what we were doing.'

Justin, incidentally, doesn't appear to consider his image or performance to be camp. 'People who call me camp are male,' he told the website uk-fusion.com. 'There's a correlation between how male you are, and how jealous you are.'

The Darkness scored their greatest hit yet with the single 'Growing On Me'. While the Top Ten remained elusive, Justin declared that sitting at Number 11 was, 'like having two Number Ones'. The band celebrated with London and Birmingham shows supporting the ancient rockers Deep Purple and Lynyrd Skynyrd at arenas, including their first addictive taste of Wembley.

They made their most talked-about appearance thus far at the Glastonbury Festival on 27 June. True to form, they arrived in a helicopter to play the opening 10 a.m. slot on the event's first day. In fact they had turned up nail-bitingly late in a 'copter with just one engine, but the assembled masses were oblivious of this panic as Justin shimmied on stage. 'Gimme a D!' he hollered. 'Gimme an 'Arkness!' He later described the show as 'brilliant. It was a real honour and a privilege opening it and we really put on a good show. Who gives you rock before breakfast? The Darkness.' After their performance, the band bravely underwent twelve hours of promotional work and drinking. A TV interview with the presenter Colin Murray, late in the day, saw them splendidly inebriated, exhibiting 'boozy Tourette's', as they would put it.

On 7 July, *Permission To Land* finally appeared on the nation's shop racks, only to be snatched off by what was now a multilayered national following, comprising people from almost all walks of life. It was appropriate that an album driven by such creative willpower should capture the imagination of so many diverse listeners. While anyone who had bought the band's three singles would have already heard 50 per cent of the songs, there was no denying that this was an incredibly strong collection of music. Adding to the album's strength was its brevity. Resisting the current trend of packing a CD up to its full running time with filler tracks, Justin and co. simply delivered ten top-notch tunes, clocking in at 39 minutes. For the most part it was a bouncy feel-good record – something very welcome in a world awaiting terrorist reprisals. The album's closing song, 'Holding My Own', was an epic

Queenesque ballad. While some reviewers commented that its seriousness seemed out of place, perhaps they hadn't considered the potential innuendo of the title and indeed the line, 'I don't need your permission to take this matter in my own two hands …'

The reviews accompanying the album's release were almost universally positive, occasionally to the extent of ranting. *Kerrang!* felt so strongly about the album that it was awarded the full five-K rating and declared 'a gleaming diamond, bobbing to the surface in an ocean of enervating, dreary shit'. The Darkness themselves, furthermore, were remarkably dubbed 'the greatest rock 'n' roll band of the last 20 years'. *Metal Hammer* noted that The Darkness 'blow away all the whiney crap; all the knowing crap and all the solemn crap that has plagued the genre of late', describing the record itself as 'very nearly a perfect stadium rock album'. The *NME* offered backhanded compliments in saying that *Permission* was 'bovine, utterly backward-looking and will probably be nothing more than an amusing footnote in musical history, but so what? Just because it's essentially heavy metal karaoke, doesn't mean you shouldn't enjoy it.'

The album's 9 July launch party at the Cross in London's King's Cross exhibited plenty of old-fashioned rock flair: plentiful booze, a giant spacecraft reflecting the album's sci-fi sleeve and some attractive young women dressed up as hostesses from The Darkness Airlines. Among the guests were Radio 1's Zoe Ball, Thin Lizzy's Scott Gorham (which especially thrilled Dan, given his by-now inexhaustible supply of Lizzy T-shirts), fellow Suffolk rockers 'A' and US chart-botherers Wheatus. While Justin joked that he was perturbed by the guests in the VIP area being more famous than he was, if the band threw a similar party now in 2004, it would be filled wall to wall with supermodels, A-list celebs and possibly even royalty.

*Permission To Land* shot straight to Number 2 in the UK album charts, pipped to the post by Beyoncé Knowles's Dangerously In Love album. Dan quipped, 'To be behind Beyoncé is the best position in the whole world!' The Darkness weren't there for long. After shifting 100,000 copies in a fortnight the album struck Number 1, where it would remain for weeks. After two months, it had sold 600,000 copies, making it double-platinum in the UK – a feat that Coldplay took four months to achieve.

Justin could see why this was happening. 'People are f*****g bored shitless with miserable rock bands and bland pop,' he told *Bang*. 'It's emotion. I call it *yearning*. Yearning for fun.'

Somewhere amid the mayhem came an invitation for The Darkness to support Robbie Williams at Knebworth Park between 1 and 3 August. Most bands would have leaped at the chance like a pack of Black Shucks, but The Darkness initially had their doubts. 'When we were asked to play,' Dan would admit, 'we were fighting this battle to be taken seriously. And the most classic example of someone doing rock in an ironic way is Robbie Williams.'

So, then, perhaps they should give it a miss. Stay at home. Not give the press more to carp on about.

'Then we heard we'd be playing to three hundred and seventy-five thousand people …'

*'Who gives you rock before breakfast?'*

# Chapter 10
# SING WHEN YOU'RE RIFFING

'Gimme a K … silent! Gimme a "Nebworth!"'

Justin Hawkins was hopping around like some mischievous satyr on Robbie Williams's ego ramp. This lengthy, somewhat phallic platform penetrated the 125,000-strong gathering at Knebworth Park. Justin probably wasn't supposed to be using the ramp, but to plonk him on a stage with such a device was tantamount to leaving Ozzy Osbourne in a room with some tasty-looking bats.

When Justin enquired whether the sea of heads before him might prefer the 'clean' or 'dirty' version of the next song, the predictable response came back like a tornado. 'Get Your Hands Off My Woman' launched in all its unflinchingly explicit glory, much to the horror of the elder members of several thousand families.

Despite initial disagreements within their ranks – Dan and Ed voted against playing here – The Darkness ultimately couldn't resist the opportunity to annex Knebworth, any more than they would resist turning up to the site in a stretch limousine with a gaggle of dolly birds. Besides the sheer volume of the event's attendance, the band were savvy enough to know that it included demographics they needed to impress. 'Robbie's got a five-to-ninety-five-year-old fan base,' explained Dan, 'and that's the appeal we're aiming to achieve.'

The band's heady combination of high-quality rock, unhinged exuberance, crowd participation and moonwalking earned huge roars of approval from the bedazzled early-afternoon crowd, who literally gave them the thumbs-up they desired. The next morning, the *Sun*'s Bizarre column incredibly ran a live colour photograph of Justin, with the headline JUSTIN IS PRINCE OF DARKNESS. 'Next time around,' raved the blurb, 'they could be headlining. They are rock nobility in the making!'

Once again, The Darkness had stepped up a notch. Knebworth had already achieved much for them and there were still two days to go. Backstage, the band made the most of their space. Justin revelled in the luxury of having a whole rack of potential costumes to wear each day, so he could stroke his chin and ponder which one to choose. The leopardskin one-piece catsuit? The pink skin-tight trousers? The fringed white jumpsuit with sequins? Among his favourite accessories was a thick white leather belt bearing the legend LOWESTOFT. 'When it comes to the crunch, you have to be proud of where you come from,' he told *Word*. 'It's all very well Eminem and D12 going on about Detroit. You have to be a bit braver to go around singing the praises of Lowestoft.'

After their second Knebworth performance – which was still triumphant but saw the crowd a tad subdued by the heat – Justin received a hug and a slap on the back from Robbie Williams himself. 'I went to say thanks,' Justin told the *Guardian*. 'He let me through his entourage of security and said …. he was a big fan of our stuff, but he didn't bother to watch us.' The next day, Justin's and Robbie's eyes met once again. This time, however, the King of Pop was more standoffish. 'He was in catering with Mark Owen and his other celeb mates, so he was a bit cooler. To be fair, I don't know if he really knew us from Adam.'

Around the time The Darkness laid waste to Hertfordshire, their album had been nominated for a Mercury Music Prize, alongside the likes of Radiohead and Coldplay. As the recipient of this award is determined by industry people, the band appeared to rank it lowly on their list of things to think about. Said Justin, 'If we won, I'd think, Ooh, that's twenty grand. Manager takes their bit, four grand each, that's oysters and champagne for two weeks.' Dan added, 'It'd just about pay for the suits we'd pay to accept it.' In the end, none of that was necessary, as the prize was trousered by Brit rapper Dizzee Rascal.

The DVDs smashed and splintered as they struck the German motorway. A few weeks into August, during a mini-tour supporting Meat Loaf, Ed Graham was demonstrating to the tour bus driver that messing with The Darkness was unwise. 'We had the hottest tour bus known to man,' Ed would relate. 'The driver could have turned the air conditioning on, but he deliberately didn't because it uses up fuel.'

Upon realising this, Ed repeatedly smashed one of the driver's PlayStation controllers against the wall, then set to work on the DVDs. 'What he gained in petrol allowance,' noted the sticksman, 'he lost in DVDs and controllers.'

In the grand scheme of rock destruction and debauchery, this was clearly not on a par with Led Zeppelin's drummer John Bonham driving a motorbike around hotel corridors. Either bad-boy behaviour wasn't in The Darkness's DNA, or they kept it ingeniously under wraps. Later in the year, Justin would admit to tugging a button from Ed's coat during an argument, which led to the banning of Aftershock on their bus. Yes, these men were animals.

On 21 August, The Darkness scooped two honours at the *Kerrang!* Awards – Best Live Act and Best Album – which salved any disappointment they might have felt over the Mercury Prize. Even the normally cocksure Justin had to concede that winning Best Album for your debut was 'insane'. Barfly's promoter Be Rozzo was present at a pre-awards live set that the band played at Tottenham Court Road's Virgin Megastore. 'I was looking around the place and saw fourteen-year-old skater kids, eighteen-year-old secretaries in high-heeled shoes, taxi drivers. What the f**k was going on here? The audience wasn't just metal kids – it was guys in suits. The cross-section of people was incredible.'

One splendidly apocryphal tale from around this time saw The Darkness allegedly being approached by some shady characters, who offered them

literally bagloads of cash to play a boat off the coast of Ibiza. After giving the matter due consideration, band and management perhaps wisely made their excuses and turned the nice, scary men down.

On 16 September, *Permission To Land* was released in America. The Darkness paid their third visit to the country – this time, not solely to play shows. They had a new record label to visit. As they entered Atlantic's New York offices, the staff afforded them a wild round of applause. 'That was a bit Spinal Tap,' Justin confessed to *Q*. 'But there's a real buzz about us here.' The band then accepted a challenge from the US magazine Blender, who gave them $800 to spend however they liked. Promptly hiring a donkey, they draped it with Darkness T-shirts and paraded the no doubt bewildered beast around outside New York's Fashion Week event. 'I don't know why we chose a donkey,' Frankie would muse to the *Guardian*. 'There's probably something subliminal about that.'

The Darkness played New York's Bowery Ballroom venue on 18 September, where they would spend hours backstage 'shitting it', prior to the show. Two-fifths of the five hundred available tickets had been allocated to the guest list, leading touts to ask in excess of $300 for spares. 'Our tour manager was offered four hundred dollars from a fan to get in,' laughed Dan, 'and he didn't take it. I almost fired him when I found out – that's almost one hundred dollars each!'

Remarkably, around half of the people in the ballroom crowd were British, including a few who had jetted from the UK especially for this show. During the set, which now included a nearly unrecognisable cover of Radiohead's 'Street Spirit (Fade Out)', Justin joked to the crowd, 'In the first two hours, we've sold fourteen copies of the album! We're taking over!' Afterwards, however, East West's managing director Korda Marshall had a new perspective on the band's Stateside chances. 'We thought they could sell maybe half a million here,' he told Q. 'But after the meetings I've had today, I think they could do 10 million in the US alone. There's no limit.' Next day, the show garnered a fairly enthusiastic *New York Times* review, which noted that Justin had 'the moves of a narcissistic rock star, no more or less self-parodic than his 70s idols'.

On 22 September, the rereleased and rerecorded 'I Believe In a Thing Called Love' single hit the UK, destined for Number 2 in the charts. That night, The Darkness were in Los Angeles, playing another show at the Roxy. This time, of course, the locals were far more excited. The show had sold out three weeks in advance and among the attendants were Ozzy Osbourne's son Jack, Blink 182 and the Bloodhound Gang. A reviewer from the *LA Times* was less taken with the band than his East Coast counterpart, preferring the band's weightier tunes to the 'shallow' 'Givin' Up'. 'At its best,' he wrote, 'The Darkness was a riff-churning monster in the AC/DC tradition … but the heavier the sound, the far better the results.'

While in town, Justin spoke to a *Sun* journalist for what would become a centre-page spread in the paper back home, with a mocked-up shot of the band holding a Union Flag in front of the Hollywood Hills. 'America is the place for girls throwing themselves at you,' Justin said. 'There's girls shaking your hand and saying, "Where are you going home tonight?" and that's their opening gambit. It's blatant.' He added, 'You have to throw them off the scent – Sue keeps an eye on me.'

While Dan revealed that the band members presently were earning only £250 a week, Justin noted, 'We could feasibly retire in six months on what we'll earn. That's realistic – I will be a millionaire this time next year, no doubt about it.'

While the band seemed to have a good chance of tickling America's fancy, it was a completely different territory from the UK. For years, British bands had attempted to conquer the States, but mostly ended up coming home defeated due to its sheer vastness. A dedicated US tour would take a band several months. The last British rock group to make a real impression in America were the post-grungers Bush. Nevertheless, The Darkness felt they could do it. 'We're gonna spend a lot of time there,' pledged Dan. 'Not many bands really get a shot at America, a proper shot, but we're really gonna go for it. As long as it takes.' Typically fearless, Justin declared that taking America would be 'slightly easier' than their achievements to date. 'I know that sounds ridiculous. It's just that there'll be a lot more touring, but that touring will stick and we'll get more for our money. Just from the experience of having gone over there and doing the odd show that's gone up like a sky rocket, it's quite apparent that what we do will be welcomed on a different level to what it has been here.'

Must Destroy's Ian Johnsen noted, 'In America they don't have this culture of despising success, and this band really work hard. All these indie no-marks go on about breaking America but they do one show in New York, don't like the drugs and want to go home. You've got to go out there and do the f*****g work and that's what The Darkness will do.'

*Jackass* star Bam Margera also predicted that The Darkness would 'blow America apart'. Yet some were a little more cautious. South by Southwest's Craig Stewart's only reservation was wondering where the band would fit into the rigid categories of US radio. 'It's a noodle scratcher!' he said. 'I'm really curious. I hope they don't end up being marginalised as some kind of hipster band. It would take a music director with some balls to add them and see what the public thinks about them.' In November, it would become apparent that 'I Believe In a Thing Called Love' was the most requested track on New York's highly influential K-Rock radio station. Clearly, their music director had the requisite testicular girth. 'American radio is waking up to The Darkness,' said Justin, 'and it's superb. They seem blown away by the fun and enjoyment factor.' The news that the band's music was set to be used on the 2004 instalment of the hugely successful *John Madden Football* US console game series further suggested that Atlantic's magic was starting to open doors.

On 7 October, Justin recorded some new vocals for a 'clean' US version of *Permission To Land*. In order to sell millions of records in America, bands need to be stocked by the massive chain stores Wal-Mart and K-Mart. To achieve this, they need a version of their CD that these prudish retail titans will accept. It's a line toed by even the rebellious Marilyn Manson and Eminem and The Darkness followed suit. Justin took advantage of the situation's comic possibilities – replacing, for instance, the 'Black Shuck' chorus line 'That dog don't give a f**k' with 'That dog don't give a duck'. While he informed one journalist that the song's closing 'Woof!' had been replaced with 'Quack!', this was possibly mere jest.

The Darkness returned to the UK to find that their profile had risen dramatically. As Justin put it, 'Blokes in white vans are shouting, "Hey, there's that c**t from The Darkness!" ' On 30 September at London's Brixton Academy, the band played a blinding performance at MTV2's fifth-birthday celebrations, alongside Jane's Addiction, the Music, the Thrills and the Rapture. The Barfly's promoter Be Rozzo recalls, 'It was f*****g unbelievable. When they came on, everyone had their hands up in the air and the whole room was going absolutely mental. The Darkness blew the roof off the place –

'I will be a *millionnaire* this time next year, no doubt about it'
**JUSTIN**

even Jane's Addiction couldn't get it close to the same temperature. I realised that this band were communicating with people on every level.' That night, Rozzo spoke to a publisher who had passed on the band the previous year. 'She hasn't recouped on all the stuff she's signed,' he says, 'and she told me, "I saw them, I passed on them and I'd still pass on them today." I looked at her and said, "Are you sure about that?" You just know that, deep down inside, she really regrets it.'

The Darkness's relentless schedule included the shooting of another outlandish video, this time for their marvellously titled forthcoming Christmas single, 'Christmas Time (Don't Let the Bells End)'. The festive rock single had been a lesser-spotted notion in recent decades, but the likes of Slade and Wizzard issued them to great success in the seventies. 'It's an art form in itself,' Justin has said. 'If you do it right, you'll end up with something really, really special. Our single will be the gift that keeps on giving, year in, year out. It's about not being with your partner for most of the year, and making the most of the holiday season together.'

After playing around in all that snow, The Darkness plunged into another extensive UK tour. Despite the incredible high they were experiencing, you could only wonder how long it might be before fatigue began to set in. Sure enough, during these dates the first cracks appeared. After a comparatively lacklustre show at Leeds's Metropolitan University, before which the band had enjoyed little sleep, Frankie told *The Face*, 'We've been trying to live the rock 'n' roll lifestyle. That's why we're f****d.'

Come mid-October, the band cancelled a show in Folkestone. The following day, Justin posted a message on their website: 'I would like to offer my sincerest apologies for what happened last night – it's the first time we've ever had to pull a show and nobody could be more disappointed than me.' The Darkness then pulled two more dates, in Liverpool and Portsmouth. Despite a horrendous *Daily Star* scare story involving cancer, Justin had been diagnosed as having laryngitis, swollen vocal chords and an infected voice box.

Thankfully, everyone's favourite screamer was back in action for the tour's final date, at London's legendary Carling Apollo. Despite being visibly nervous about losing his voice again, Justin heroically led his band through a blinder, made all the more special by the venue's history. Formerly known as the Hammersmith Odeon, it was once immortalised by Motörhead's *No Sleep Til Hammersmith* live album. Indeed, as The Darkness played, the final power chord from the previous night's AC/DC show was still reverberating around in the rafters.

Whereas some frontmen might have modestly burbled about how they'd never *dreamed* of treading these boards, Justin didn't bother. He'd always known he would tread them. The frontman did, however, find himself making an announcement that he could never have predicted: 'I don't have cancer and I never said I did!' In publicly denouncing a tabloid tale, Justin Hawkins had truly joined the higher echelons of rock stardom.

*'Our [Christmas] single
will be the gift that
keeps on giving'*

JUSTIN

*The Darkness's*
*ambitions are legion*

# Epilogue
# DANGER! DANGER!

The music business can do very strange things to people – and, if you're in a rock 'n' roll band, you're all the more likely to be on the receiving end. As rock stars' egos, livers and wallets expand, while their friends, wives and septums vanish altogether, they start to adopt a rather skewed view of the world. Before you know it, they're burrowing their faces into mountains of cocaine and firing massive machine guns about the place.

Talking to *The Face* in October, Justin himself seemed to suggest that intraband relations had already undergone a subtle transformation. 'We all used to go out to the pub together,' he said. 'Then I stopped. I decided to become elusive, enigmatic and untouchable.'

When asked if he thought The Darkness would split up, and whether he'd be the cause, he said, 'Yes. Undoubtedly. It happens to all bands. Things have already gone that way, to an extent.' He then claimed that he would fake his own death and be lowered into his own funeral in a cube of formaldehyde. Which rather diluted the entire statement's credibility. That Justin Hawkins is a slippery one.

James Leah harbours few worries about how his old friend will handle success. 'The only time I'd be worried would be if Justin didn't want to be my friend any more. He's shown no signs of that so far, but he is becoming more insular. I can see that he doesn't trust some people around him very much. To some extent, that's a healthy paranoia. He's got lots of people in bands continually emailing him, asking for help.'

Leah paints the post-success Justin as 'a really intelligent bloke who picks up things really quickly, but has doubts about who his real friends are. I know people who think the world of Justin and would do anything for him, but, because they weren't around when The Darkness began, I sometimes get the impression that he doesn't necessarily trust their motives.' Leah's only other concern is that 'Justin will become a millionaire and then spend it all – he's not great with money. He might spend it all on renovating Bungay Castle or something!'

The promoter Valerie Gayrimond says, 'Some people just see the tip of The Darkness's iceberg and think they're an overnight success, but they've really hung in there. They worked hard to put on a good show and Justin did a lot of work to improve himself. That doesn't happen in a week. They're as equipped for success as anyone can be.'

'Success has brought a certain amount of responsibility,' Justin has told *Q*. 'I've met fans of the band who tell us we've changed their lives and not just because they have our names tattooed on their arms. The responsibility can be overwhelming, and that's why it's important to still do normal things from time to time. Like go swimming.'

As long as Justin finishes seemingly serious comments with a quirky punchline, we'll know he's all right. Last word on this topic goes to South by Southwest's Craig Stewart, who has an eminently sensible point to make. 'It seems like The Darkness thought they were megastars all along,' he says. 'So all of this is not much of a leap.'

The Darkness's ambitions are legion. Some of them are also preposterous. Justin wants the newly rebuilt Wembley Stadium to be renamed The Darkness Stadium. 'We'll play there,' he informed the *Guardian*. 'I'll be fired onstage as a human cannonball. I'll hit the wall, slide down and start the first track.' They'd also like to 'create a whole new race of super-nerds', due to the fact that their audience is half bookworms, half supermodels. 'They'll soon start breeding kids,' mused Frankie, 'who are hyperintelligent, very self-conscious, but gorgeous with really long legs.'

Then there are the less tongue-in-cheek goals. 'I want fifty articulated trucks and a huge stage,' Dan told *Metal Hammer*. 'That is a genuine ambition and I think we can do it – although it might not be until our second album.'

Ah, that second album. 'It's going to be f*****g great,' Dan has enthused, while innocently making a rod for his own back. 'Ten times bigger and better than the first one. We've got a long career ahead of us.'

'People think we'll be gone in six months,' Justin has said, 'but just wait – we'll be conquering Andorra by then.' Some might not believe him. Then again, if such doubters had attended Kirkley High School in 1990 and a funny-looking kid in an Aerosmith T-shirt had introduced himself with 'I'm Justin Hawkins and I'm going to be a rock star,' they might have laughed in his face.

Who'd be laughing now?